On the Sidelines: Decisions, Skills, and Training in

On the Sidelines: Decisions, Skills, and Training in Youth Sports

How to Help Your Child Grow Through Sports

JON C. HELLSTEDT, Ph.D.
DANIEL S. ROOKS, M.S.
and
DAVID G.A. WATSON, M.D.

(with editorial assistance from Virginia M. Kimball)

Foreword by Lyle J. Micheli, M.D., Director of Sports
Medicine, the Children's Hospital, Boston, Massachusetts

Editor: Linda K. Fuller, Ph.D.

Production by: The Magazine Group

First Edition
First Printing, March 1988

ISBN 0-87425-067-6
Copyright 1988

Published by
HRD Press
22 Amherst Rd.
Amherst, MA 01002

TO OUR FAMILIES
PAST, PRESENT, AND FUTURE
WITH WHOM WE HAVE SHARED
THOSE SPECIAL MOMENTS
ON THE SIDELINES

Table of Contents

Foreword

It must be evident to even the most casual observer that we are in the midst of a sports and exercise boom in this country. Americans of all shapes, sizes, and ages are pursuing new or renewed interests in sports as diverse as tennis, gymnastics, and rugby.

Children are also included in this trend, and yet there is growing concern that children today are less fit than previous generations; that they score lower on physical performance tests; and that the incidence of childhood and adolescent obesity is significantly greater than ten years ago. The crux of this controversy is what is the best way for our children to obtain healthy exercise: from organized sports programs, from playground sports activities, from school-based physical education curricula, or simply, from more walking?

While children have been involved in play and sports since time immemorial, organized sports for children, with teams, leagues, and tournaments, are really of recent vintage. Beginning post–World War II in the United States, this trend has since spread to the rest of the world. The growth of competitive sports for children has not been without its critics, however. In 1959 the American Academy of Pediatrics released a position statement recommending that therre be no competitive sports for children under the age of fourteen. In the ensuing years, other medical societies in other nations echoed this stand. These interdictions, by and large, have gone unheeded. I am convinced that, for a variety of reasons, organized sports for children are with us to stay. If anything, this trend will grow. Therefore, it becomes the task of all of us who deal with sports, exercise, and children, and who care about the well-being of our children, to see that organized sports competitions for children are done well and safely.

Proponents of organized children's sports argue that children enjoy sports more when organized, that skill acquisition is more rapid and efficient, that sports are safer with adult supervision, and that it is a much more efficient way to use limited recreational facilities. Critics argue that organized sports expose certain children to excessive psychological stress, with resultant harm. They also note that there is no evidence that the overall rate of injury in children's sports is less, particularly when overuse injuries are taken into account. Overuse injuries, the result of repetitive microtrauma, such as the torque of overhand throwing, or the footfall of running, were rarely encountered in children until the advent of organized, repetitive sports training in this age group. Finally, these critics contend that there is no convincing evidence that children enjoy sports more in the competitive arena than they do in a free play situation.

As a sports medicine practitioner, with a particular interest in children's sports, I have often been asked to arbitrate between opponents and proponents of organized sports competitions for children. When asked which sport is safe for children, at what age, or which sport is unsafe, my answer is invariably the same. In any sports program, the quality of adult supervision and parental interaction is the prime determinant of the safety or advisability of a given sports program. Thus, in a given community with poor adult supervision and interaction, soccer may be a very unhealthy and dangerous sport for a boy or girl, while in another community, with proper adult supervision and interaction, Pop Warner football may be safe and beneficial to young participants. Additionally, with proper preparation and proper attention to conditioning and progression of training, most injuries, physical or psychological, are preventable in this age group.

There are three major factors that determine the success of a given sports program for a given child: The child, and in particular whether he or she has been matched to a proper sport; the parent; and the coach. The authors of On the Sidelines, have addressed all three of these factors, from the viewpoint of the parent. They have attempted to explore the opportunities and challenges of present-day youth sports. While stating clearly that they are proponents of organized sports for children, they dramatically detail the pitfalls of an organized sports program where child, parent, and coach have not coordinated their efforts, and their goals.

The first portion of the text outlines in clear, simple language the psychological factors at work when children and their families enter the organized sports system. It enables parents to assess their present role in their child's sports participation, and provides valuable insight into the dynamics of this process.

The second section outlines the dynamics of growth and development of children, and clearly demonstrates the impact that physical activities can have on this process. It provides the parents with an assessment program that enables them, and their children, to monitor changes in fitness or performance over time. While this assessment is no substitute for a formal fitness assessment by health professionals, the data obtained can provide valuable information not only for parent and child, but also for the health professional, whether family physician or pediatrician, who is caring for the child.

The final section details a safe and effective exercise program that can be used by parent and child to help prevent injury in sports and enhance performance. Again, as the authors caution, this program is dependent upon proper supervision by health professionals or exercise specialists. Most importantly, this section promotes a clear understanding of the principles of fitness exercises by the parents, which help them determine whether their child is receiving proper adult supervision and coaching.

In summary, then, the authors have combined their diverse but complementary talents to produce a truly unique work. This is the first sports book that outlines in a clear, comprehensive, and easily readable style, for the parent, the often complex interplay of psychological, developmental, and physical factors when a child participates in organized sports programs. I recommend this text without reservation to every parent. I particularly recommend it to parents who willingly, or unwillingly, are now cast in the role of the "sports parent."

> *Lyle J. Micheli, M.D.*
> Director of Sports Medicine
> Children's Hospital
> Boston, Massachusetts

About the Authors

JON C. HELLSTEDT teaches in the Psychology Department at the University of Lowell and has a clinical practice in Westford, Massachusetts. His interests are in marriage and family counseling, interpersonal communication, and sport psychology. He has counseled athletes and their families for many years and has worked with ski racers on mental preparation for competition. He is president of the Sugarloaf Mountain Ski Club. Jon and his wife Sharon enjoy skiing, tennis, and watching their five children participate in skiing, soccer, tennis, basketball, and gymnastics events.

DANIEL S. ROOKS is a doctoral candidate at Boston University. He is director of the CHAMPS Program in the Division of Sports Medicine at the Children's Hospital in Boston. As an exercise physiologist, his primary interests focus on the contribution physiological assessment and conditioning play in injury prevention and enhanced sports performance. He has counseled athletes of all ages, but continues to concentrate the majority of his work on children at all levels of competition. He and his wife Betsy enjoy running, weight training, skiing, and tennis. They live in Marblehead, Massachusetts, with their Newfoundland dog Samson.

DAVID G.A. WATSON grew up in Australia, where he attended medical school and participated in many sports including rugby, golf, cricket, tennis, track, and scuba diving. He later received postgraduate training in London and at the Children's Hospital Medical Center in Boston. He lives in Westford, Massachusetts, where he has an active private practice in pediatrics. He is the team physi-  cian for Westford Academy, Nashoba Valley Technical High School, and the Westford Lions Pop Warner football team. He and his wife Susan have two children and are enjoying some new challenges including skiing and windsurfing.

VIRGINIA KIMBALL is a freelance journalist who writes news and feature stories for a daily newspaper, magazine articles, and stories and plays for children. She and her husband Dean live in Westford, Massachusetts, and are the parents of nine children who have been active in many sports.

Acknowledgments

The authors would like to express our appreciation to the following who have made this book possible:

- Virginia Kimball, for bringing our three approaches together and giving the text one voice, and for keeping us focused during many phases of this project.
- Linda K. Fuller, our editor at HRD Press, whose firm direction has energized us.
- our spouses and children, who have loved and supported us during this collaboration.
- the more than thousand young athletes and their families with whom we have worked, who have stimulated so many of the ideas expressed in this book.
- The North Shore Jewish Community Center for their cooperation and use of their facilities. We also thank Jim Koepfler for his photography in chapters 5 and 6 and Rachel Haskin, Jeffrey Schwartz, Peter Rooks, Jared Rooks, and Jennifer Rooks for serving as models.
- and the many friends and colleagues who have helped by reading and commenting on the manuscript, including Dr. Kenneth Erickson, Lois Erickson, Dr. Kathy Hulbert, Dr. Anne Mulvey, Dr. Lyle J. Micheli, and Professor Claire Chamberlin.

We would also like to thank the following people and organizations for granting us permission to quote from their work:

- David Bushnell, Acton, Massachusetts, for portions of "Burnout: Too Much, Too Soon."
- The American Alliance for Health, Physical Education, Recreation, and Dance, 2900 Association Drive, Reston, Virginia 22091, which has given us permission to reprint portions of its publications.
- Ross Laboratories, 625 Cleveland Avenue, Columbus, Ohio, 43125, for permission to use height, weight, and pubertal development charts.
- Macmillan Publishing Company, 866 Third Avenue, New York, New York 10022, for permission to reprint data from Cantu, Robert (ed.), *Clinical Sports Medicine* (Macmillan, 1984).
- *World Tennis* magazine, for giving permission to quote directly from Jim Loehr's article, "The Pressure Cooker."

On the Sidelines: Decisions, Skills, and Training in Youth Sports

Introduction

Are *you* an "athletic family"?

If you wonder whether or not you are an athletic family, try answering the following questions.

Do you spend much of your free time on the sidelines watching your children's games?

Do you spend what you consider to be a large percentage of your money on sports equipment, entry and training fees, sports travel, sports camps, private coaching, and seasonal gifts for your children's coaches?

Does your family have difficulty deciding which recreational program to choose, such as playing spring baseball or soccer?

Is sport participation an important part of your daily or weekly schedule?

Do you enjoy competing in adult recreational activities?

Have you had to choose between a playoff game or other athletic event and a family vacation?

How are your children's rooms decorated? What pictures and posters hang on the walls? Are there sports posters? Are there trophies and ribbons?

If you answered yes to any one of these questions, chances are that you are an athletic family!

An *athletic family* is a household in which a large percentage of the members' time, money, and emotional energy is focused on the children's sports activities. It's hectic getting up early or staying up late to take a child to practice; shopping for new athletic shoes every season; racing from softball practice to skating lessons; losing the announcements that coaches send home; clenching your jaw when your ten-year-old can't find his or her soccer shirt; looking for more tennis balls. And the expense of it often leads you to ask, Is it worth it?

Many parents feel the joy—and the tension—of being an athletic family. They want to know how to keep it all in balance. They would like to know the long-range effects of the many decisions that have to be made.

This book will help you learn to balance the demands and get the benefits of being an athletic family. It is written for the parents who participate on the sidelines or sit in the bleachers and cheer for a peewee soccer or baseball player, young gymnast, ski racer, or mature varsity athlete.

The authors of this book all work professionally with athletic families. One is a pediatrician, another a sport psychologist, and the other an exercise physiologist. We are athletes ourselves. We all participate in sports now as we did when we were in high school and college. Two of us are parents of athletic children; the third is recently married.

In our lives and work we have seen the benefits of youth sports for children and their families. We have witnessed the joys of learning skills and achieving goals. Our own families and those with whom we have worked have been enriched by these experiences.

But we've also seen the problems: children harmed physically and/or emotionally from too much parental pressure; unnecessary injuries from poor guidance or improper training; family relations strained because of the pressures of sports involvement. Despite the potential problems, we continue to believe in the beneficial value of athletics for children.

The availability and popularity of youth sports present new questions for parents. Many of them are asking themselves such questions as,

- How much time, money, and energy should we invest in youth sports?
- What is my role as a parent in my child's sports?
- At what age should a child participate in competitive sports?
- Should I help motivate my child, and if so, how can I help?
- Is it a good idea to coach my own child?

These questions will be answered by the psychologist on our team in chapters 1, 3, and 4.

Parents also wonder about their child's potential talent. They ask,

- What physical characteristics does my child possess in sports?
- Given my child's size, body structure, reaction time, coordination, and muscle strength, what sports are best for my child?
- Is my child an early or late maturer? How do I determine this?

The pediatrician on our team will answer these questions in chapter 2.

Parents also question the value of weight and conditioning training. This is a new area of development, and many parents are asking,

- Is weight training helpful?
- Does it help prevent injuries?
- When should a child start to weight train?
- How can I help my child do it safely?
- What is the proper nutrition for a young athlete?

The exercise physiologist will answer these questions and more in chapters 5 and 6.

In the chapters to follow we have drawn together our knowledge and experience in working with children and parents. We hope the unique combination of information from different viewpoints will help you deal with some of the difficult questions and dilemmas that you face as a parent of athletic children.

Before reading further, take the simple quiz below. We will refer to the results later in the book.

Enjoy the journey you are about to begin!

A QUIZ FOR PARENTS

The following questions will help you assess your values in regard to youth sports. Here's how to take the quiz: Pick one of your children who is active in sports and answer the questions with reference to that child.

For example, if your oldest daughter plays tennis, answer the questions in reference to her. If the question refers to team sport and your child plays an individual sport, answer the question *as if* the situation applied to her. Circle the number or rank the item that *best* describes your attitudes and behavior. If you have two or more children involved in sports, repeat the quiz for each child.

Child's (C) Name _____ Age ____ Sport _____

1. I go to (C's) games.

Never	Occasionally	Sometimes	Frequently	Always
1	2	3	4	5

2. The most important thing for me is that (C) (rank the following according to importance, with 3 being the most important and 1 the least important):

a. _____ has fun in his/her sport.
b. _____ develops skills in his/her sport.
c. _____ is successful in his/her sport.

3. (C) senses my disapproval when he/she performs poorly in sports.

Never	Occasionally	Sometimes	Frequently	Always
1	2	3	4	5

4. The main purpose of youth sports is for (C) to have fun.

Strongly disagree	Mildly disagree	Yes and no	Mildly agree	Strongly agree
1	2	3	4	5

5. I believe it is important that (C) has a goal when participating in sports (such as making varsity, being a ranked competitor, getting a college scholarship).

Strongly disagree	Mildly disagree	Yes and no	Mildly agree	Strongly agree
1	2	3	4	5

6. The main value of youth sports is for (C) to learn certain physical skills (catching, running, skiing).

Strongly disagree	Mildly disagree	Yes and no	Mildly agree	Strongly agree
1	2	3	4	5

7. I prefer that (C) work with a coach who emphasizes (rank as in question 2):

a. _____ having fun in his/her sport.
b. _____ developing skills in his/her sport.
c. _____ being a winner in his/her sport.

8. I am willing to make financial sacrifices so that (C) can get the best opportunities in sports.

Never	Occasionally	Sometimes	Frequently	Always
1	2	3	4	5

Instructions for Scoring

Place your answers for each item in the spaces below.

	Fun	Skills	Goals	Involvement
				1. _____
	2a. _____	2b. _____	2c. _____	
				3. _____
	4. _____			
			5. _____	
		6. _____		
	7a. _____	7b. _____	7c. _____	
				8. _____
Totals	_____	_____	_____	_____

Your Parental Profile

Now take your total scores on each dimension and place them on the chart below.

	Fun	Skills	Goals	Involvement
	11	11	11	11
High	10	10	10	10
	9	9	9	9
	8	8	8	8
Moderate	7	7	7	7
	6	6	6	6
	5	5	5	5
Low	4	4	4	4
	3	3	3	3

Draw a heavy dark line that connects the number of your score under each item. This line is your profile.

A typical scoring sheet might look like this:

	Fun	Skills	Goals	Involvement
				1. __4__
	2a. __1__	2b. __3__	2c. __2__	
				3. __3__
	4. __3__			
			5. __4__	
		6. __4__		
	7a. __2__	7b. __3__	7c. __1__	
				8. __3__
Totals	__6__	__10__	__7__	__10__

If you have scored the quiz properly, your profile sheet might look something like this:

	Fun	Skills	Goals	Involvement
	11	11	11	11
High	10	10	10	10
	9	9	9	9
	8	8	8	8
Moderate	7	7	7	7
	6	6	6	6
	5	5	5	5
Low	4	4	4	4
	3	3	3	3

This profile gives you an indication of the relative value you give to the three elements of sports (fun, skills development, and goal attainment) and your own level of personal involvement in your child's sports activities. The meaning of your profile will be discussed in chapter 1.

Chapter 1

Youth Sports and the Family: Opportunities and Challenges

by Jon C. Hellstedt, Ph.D.

The scene in the town where two of the authors live illustrates the pleasure that children and parents can derive from organized youth sports.

Saturday at the Soccer Field

From early morning until late afternoon the town recreation field is alive with activity.

On one field the six- and seven-year-olds line up for the start of the game. They use a small ball, play on a shortened field, and have small goals. Boys and girls play together, learning to respect one another. The parents on the sidelines are enjoying themselves, cheering for their children as well as the others on the team. There is some yelling, but it is mostly instructional. The expressions on the children's faces indicate they are having fun. Five minutes after the game is over, it doesn't matter who won or lost.

On another field the older boys and girls are playing on teams together. They are learning to respect each other by competing and having fun.

Later in the day, the eleven- and twelve-year-old boys are playing against a team from another town. This group, a more advanced team, is coached by a parent who has an extensive background in playing and coaching soccer. He teaches the boys the fundamentals of the game. He encourages them to play hard but to respect their opponents and treat them with dignity.

Hundreds of children, coaches, and parents are at the town field at any given time. After their games are over, hundreds more come.

This is youth sports at its best. Children are learning skills and testing their growing bodies in healthy competition, where winning is not emphasized.

In my community the most popular youth sport in the fall is soccer. Numbers speak for the success of the program. A total of 1,025 children aged six to nineteen, representing close to 50 percent of the school-age population, participate.

Youth participation in sports such as soccer has grown dramatically in the last two decades. Two psychologists who have done extensive research on youth sports, Frank Smoll and Richard Smith (1977), estimate that twenty million children between the ages of seven and eighteen participate in sports programs. The large number of children participating in competitive sports raises many questions and poses many challenges.

EMERGENCE OF THE ATHLETIC FAMILY

The growth in youth sports has resulted in increasing family involvement. If Smoll and Smith's figures are accurate, on the sidelines are somewhere between twenty-five million and thirty-five million parents watching their children participate. The fact is, as children spend more time in sports, so do many parents. Mom or Dad may help as coaches, volunteers, sponsors, or fundraisers. Attending games becomes a regular weekend activity for many families, sometimes even including the dog! If two or three children are involved, parents may spend most of the day, and in some cases the entire weekend, watching their children play.

Certain family structures emerge that become identified with a particular sport. In a given community, for example, there can be soccer families, baseball families, or hockey families.

THE VALUE OF THE ATHLETIC FAMILY

There are three predominant results that participation in sports produces for both individuals and families: fun, skills development, and the accomplishment of goals.

As parents we think about how we can keep our children interested in what we do as a family. Having fun together is a key ingredient. Fun is something that keeps family members involved in family activities. So is learning how to do new things. Learning is a process of developing new skills that result in an inner feeling of competence.

For many families, however, stagnation and boredom can become problems. Children and parents complain that they never do anything fun together. Children in stagnant families do one of two things: either they move outward, seeking enjoyment outside the family, or they move deeper into themselves.

The members of the families who go outward lose important connections with one another. The children seek fun away from home. They do not enjoy being with their parents. They would rather be at someone else's house or at another meeting place to socialize with their peers.

When family members move inward, they lose contact with outside stimulation. Without learning new skills, these families frequently experience boredom. Fun becomes an evening in front of the television watching a collection of movies rented from the video store. They stop learning new skills from exposure to outside activities.

Participation in athletics can offer a solution to both forms of family stagnation. Sports provide a family with an opportunity to join together in common activities, and allow its members to make meaningful connections with people and activities beyond the family. Most important, sports provide a context for opening and maintaining lines of communication between the family members.

Fun

Sports are an extension of play. All organized sports have their origin in the games children play.

Sports and Play

Sports and play are related. For example, I have watched the young children outside my office window play kicking games with a ball and an imaginary goal. They run relay races. Then they set up a slalom course with old bamboo stakes and pretend they are ski racing. They time each other.

The other night my ten-year-old son called me into his bedroom to show me the basketball hoop hanging on the back of his bedroom door. We played against each other with a rolled up sock wrapped with duct tape serving as a basketball. He was the offense. I was the defense.

We play a type of football game in the house in which my children try to run by a tackler and score by reaching an imaginary end zone. We call the game Hike, One, Two, Three...

Athletic families have fun. Fun is most often built around the sports they do together.

A research study involving close to a hundred fifteen-year-old ski racers (Hellstedt 1986) asked the question, "Do you have fun skiing with your parents?" Seventy-five percent answered yes. Other studies indicate that athletic families have fun together. A study of championship tennis players (Bloom 1985) indicated that much of the weekend the family would be together at the tennis court. However, the families did more than play tennis; they also played golf, biked, and skied.

If sports remain a form of play, participation can enhance relationships within the family. A parent who enjoys tennis knows the thrill of running, hitting the ball, and putting a good series of shots together. But there is something even more special about playing with your own son or daughter. Watching your child return a shot or make a good play at the net makes the whole experience more fun. The children enjoy it, too. They feel important when their parents are willing to spend this kind of time with them.

Fun generates a high level of energy within the family. This energy translates into a high-activity level. An athletic family is active. The parents often like to stay fit. A father and his daughter go out in the yard and throw a ball to each other, a mother and her son go to the tennis court to practice, or the whole family goes skiing together. Vacation time can be spent playing tennis, golf, swimming and snorkeling, or sailing a sunfish together. An action orientation keeps family energy high.

Recently there has been a lot of publicity about how the children of today are in poorer physical condition than they were some years ago. One of the reasons for this decline is that television has become a mode of entertainment for many children and adults. They come home from school or work, turn on the television, and are passively entertained. Prior to the advent of television, children would often be outside jumping rope or playing jacks, developing physical strength and eye-hand coordination. Families who emphasize sports participation help their children stay active and in better physical condition—and away from the television set.

Active families often learn to manage time effectively. Because the parents and children are busy with practices and games, other necessary activities such as studying and household chores are well planned and organized. The refrigerator or kitchen counter usually has lists of priority items to be accomplished that day or week. There is little time for boredom or time to waste.

Skills Development

If you talk to happy and successful people, one of the things they will say is that they enjoy learning new things. A healthy and mature person enjoys learning new skills. This is true for families, too. When family members learn how to ski, scuba dive, rock climb, bicycle, or play tennis, they participate in a learning environment that is stimulating.

Sports participation provides this learning environment. Parents and children can learn and practice new skills together. Parents may not be able to learn the intricate movements of a figure skater, but they can go to the rink and learn how to improve their own skating while their child trains.

Try What the Kids Do

At Sugarloaf Mountain in Maine, the Ski Club has always provided coaching and racing opportunities for the children. The role of the parents, however, was more supportive than participative. Three years ago the club began a new program—the Cardiac League. The club provided coaching and some races for the parents. Those who participated felt strongly that it improved their skiing skills and helped them appreciate the difficulties their children face as they learn racing techniques.

Sports can lead brothers and sisters to learn skills from one another. Younger siblings can often learn throwing and kicking from their older brothers and sisters. They can practice together. Going to watch each other's games helps develop bonds that are invaluable.

The skills that family members learn in sports are not just physical; skills teach how to live a mature and responsible lifestyle. Children learn from their parents. They see their parents perform a certain behavior and through repeated exposure or teaching incorporate the behavior into their own personality. Many lessons can be learned in athletic families.

Modeling Lessons

A father comes home from a tennis game with a friend. His son asks him how he played. The father says, "Not well. My serve was way off. I need to practice on my second serve."

The lesson the son learns here is one of personal responsibility for poor performance; the father is saying he is responsible for not playing well and he needs to improve the areas of his game where he is weak.

A mother sits down with her son and has him plan and make a list of goals for the week. He develops a plan for completing his schoolwork, attending his practices and the weekend game, and still participating in rehearsals for the junior choir musical at church.

The lesson learned is that sports are important but so are other things, and a balance of priorities can be maintained through planning and time management.

Another skill that can be learned in an athletic family is communication. Family intimacy can be achieved by communicating with one another on the same level of emotional expression. It can be the sharing of either positive or negative emotions. Within athletic families there are many opportunities for intimacy.

Communication Vignettes

While riding in the car a mother and daughter share the sadness of a personal or team loss. Both notice tears in the other's eyes. A warm hug or embrace shows support and affection.

A father and son stop for an ice cream cone after a soccer game. They talk about how the son feels he is playing. Dad shares his pride with his son about his developing ability.

Shopping together for that new pair of basketball shoes can be a special time—a mutual appreciation of money spent on something the child will enjoy.

An honest sharing results when a parent and child discuss the child's desire to drop out of a youth sport.

A husband and wife are brought closer to one another when they sit up late one night and share their excitement about their daughter's gymnastics.

A husband and wife share their anger and sadness over their daughter's knee injury that will require surgery.

Children also learn social and interpersonal skills through youth sports. They learn how to get along with others, how to express themselves, and how to make and keep friends. This will be discussed in more detail in chapter 3.

Goal Attainment

Doesn't it feel good when you accomplish something you have wanted to do for a long time? Remember how good you felt last autumn when you finished stacking the woodpile or wallpapering the playroom? An essential part of self-esteem is knowing you have reached a new level of accomplishment. You feel competent and secure in yourself. The sports environment is a place where a participant can learn and experience the inner joy that comes from accomplishing a goal.

To become successful in anything, we need to learn how to set goals and attain them. In athletic families goal setting becomes very important. Parents teach their child that if he or she wants to make the varsity basketball team, hard work and self-discipline are needed to work toward that goal.

Goal orientation is a great lesson that athletes can learn. The lessons learned in sports are transferable to all areas of life.

THE FAMILY BALANCE BEAM

A person who is psychologically healthy has found a balance of fun, useful skills, and the accomplishment of goals. A healthy approach to sports also requires a balance of fun, skills development, and personal success (goal attainment). If this balance is disturbed, there can be problems.

In recent years a lot of attention in the media has focused on the negative aspects of youth sports. Many newspaper and magazine articles report how children have been harmed, either physically or psychologically, by participation in youth sports.

Kids and Sports

A recent television documentary, titled *Kids and Sports* (shown on HBO in the fall of 1986), dramatically illustrated the excessive levels of personal stress that children are exposed to at an early age in sports. The program featured four children under highly stressful situations.

The first, a twelve-year-old female gymnast, was sent away from her family to live near a famous coach in order to train intensively for the next Olympics.

A young boy, whose father believed his son's financial future depended on being a top-level tennis player, was sent away from his family to live at and attend a tennis academy in Florida.

A high school quarterback, whose father has prepared him since age two or three to be a professional football player, by the age of sixteen had worked with special coaches for strength training, passing skills, and mental toughness.

The fourth, a star high school hockey goalie who doesn't achieve his ambition to be a National Hockey League star, commits suicide.

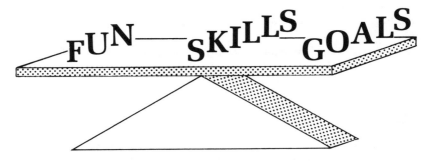

Figure 1.1 The family balance beam.

The balance beam (figure 1.1) can be easily tipped in one direction. Overzealous parents pressure their children to achieve, often at the expense of fun and enjoyment. Let us now see how tipping the balance in one direction or the other affects how parents interact with their children.

THREE TYPES OF PARENTS

Parents are the architects of the family, and their attitudes and behaviors influence the type of person and athlete their child will become. There are three types of parents: the Persuader, the Avoider, and the Enabler.

If you have not already done so, complete the Quiz for Parents in the introduction. Your own profile from the scoring of this quiz can be used to determine which of these three types fits you.

The Persuader

The Persuader puts more weight on the success end of the balance beam than on either fun or skills development. Performance becomes this parent's main concern. Will my child be the best? Will my child make the national team? Will my child get an athletic scholarship to college. The Persuader wants results.

An example of a Persuader style of parenting comes from the HBO documentary *Kids and Sports* and an article by Jack Friedman (1986) titled "Building the Perfect Player."

Building the Perfect Player

Todd's mother and father are examples of parents who put a heavy emphasis on goal attainment. Since Todd was two years old they have been grooming him to be an NFL quarterback. Marv, a former NFL lineman and strength-training coach, and Trudi, a nutritionist, have devoted their parenting to producing an outstanding athlete.

At four years Todd was developing ability on a balance beam. By the time he was eight years old he was playing organized flag football. At eleven he was sent to a vision specialist to improve reaction time. Now seventeen, Todd works out five hours a day on weight training, running, and passing skills. Marv works out with him daily (he has taken a leave of absence from his own career to devote his time to Todd's development) and has secured the services of other professionals such as a running coach, throwing coach, and strength-training coach. Trudi takes care of his nutrition and has been feeding him energy and health foods since he was a toddler.

Marv and Trudi have a clear goal. They want Todd to be an NFL quarterback. Todd wants that as a goal, too. He changed high schools to play in a better football program and has many top-level colleges scouting him. The emphasis on goal attainment has been successful. Though an NFL career remains a future unknown, he will undoubtedly play football, at full scholarship, for a leading college.

Has this been harmful to Todd? He says no. He likes the time and attention that his mother and father have given him and he shares their commitment to hard work and goal attainment. He does admit, however, that some of the fun things have suffered. He does not spend time on art and drawing, which he enjoys, and his social life has been limited because of his commitment to training.

Because they use their parental influence to keep Todd on a certain predetermined path, Marv and Trudi are examples of Persuaders. Their role is to supervise and *persuade* Todd to reach his goal. They often have to structure his time and energy toward goal attainment and away from other childlike activities.

Is this bad for Todd? An outside observer might say yes. Too much pressure. A father living out his own athletic frustrations through his son. Too much child-centeredness in the family.

There is no doubt that Marv and Trudi are overinvolved in Todd's athletics. The balance beam is dramatically tilted in one direction. An injury that might affect Todd's career could be emotionally devastating to the family because of its narrow focus and emotional involvement

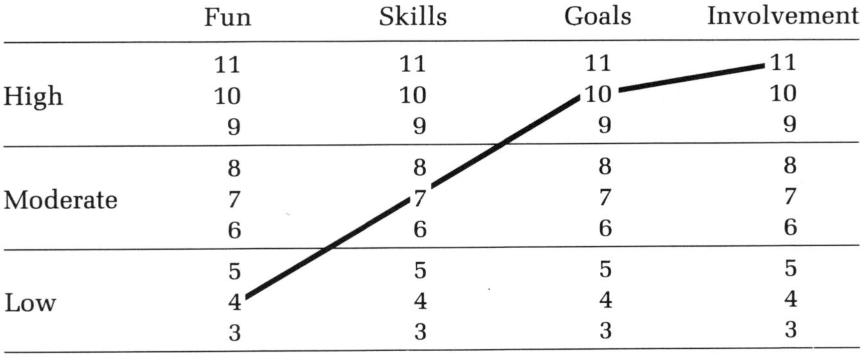

	Fun	Skills	Goals	Involvement
High	11 10 9	11 10 9	11 10 9	11 10 9
Moderate	8 7 6	8 7 6	8 7 6	8 7 6
Low	5 4 3	5 4 3	5 4 3	5 4 3

Figure 1.2   Profile of a Persuader.

in Todd's success. The balance is not there. The fun side of his life is disproportionately small.

Figure 1.2 indicates that a parent who is a Persuader has a high level of involvement. He or she goes to games, is willing to support the child's involvement financially, and is achievement-oriented. This type of parent has high expectations and expects good results from the child's performance. The Persuader believes that fun and skills development are important, but not as important as the results.

Persuaders' children are often successful, at least in the early stages. They get more opportunities, time, and parental attention at a young age. Their skills develop early, but sometimes at a price: excessive pressure due to high parental expectations.

Persuaders come in all types. Mild Persuaders are well-meaning parents who unwittingly pressure their children. They want the best for their child and like to see him or her winning. The extreme Persuaders are the ''little-league parents'' that we read about and see at some youth sports events. They are parents who get angry when their children strike out or make an error. They yell at the coaches or referees when they feel their child is wronged. They keep a list of errors the child makes in a tennis match.

The Avoider

Sports participation requires time, discipline, and self-sacrifice for goal attainment. Sports are fun, but to be good at them also requires hard work.

Avoiders are parents who view athletics as fun or play but are not willing to commit time and energy to support their children's involvement

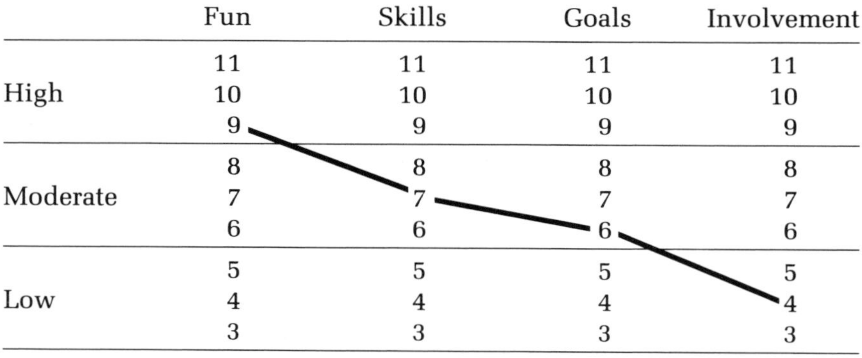

	Fun	Skills	Goals	Involvement
High	11 10 9	11 10 9	11 10 9	11 10 9
Moderate	8 7 6	8 7 6	8 7 6	8 7 6
Low	5 4 3	5 4 3	5 4 3	5 4 3

Figure 1.3 Profile of an Avoider.

in sports. Avoiders do not teach their children the self-discipline that is required to be a good athlete. They do not spend time helping them learn the necessary skills.

The profile of the Avoider (figure 1.3) is higher in fun than in either skills development or goal attainment and low in involvement.

It Keeps Them Off the Streets

Tom is an accountant who has recently left a large CPA firm and started a practice in the community where he lives. His wife Ann has recently returned to graduate school to further her education. Their children, Tommie, age twelve, and Melissa, age ten, participate in youth soccer in the fall, skiing in the winter, and tennis and swimming at a private club in the spring and summer.

Tom and Ann are both busy with their activities and often don't take time to go to the children's games. Tom doesn't get time to hit tennis balls with Tommie and Melissa. Ann attempts to play with them on occasion but she, too, is tied up with her schoolwork and other activities. The children are left on their own to practice.

Tom and Ann value their free time on weekends to entertain or spend time together. They don't spend much time with the children but value youth sports as a way to keep the children busy in an activity the children enjoy. "It keeps them off the streets," Tom will often say.

Tommie's soccer coach notes that the boy has great athletic potential but fools around too much at practice. He doesn't work hard on developing his skills or improving his ability as a soccer player. His tennis coach suggests that he ask his father to hit balls with him on weekends, but Tommie's response is, "My dad is too busy to play tennis with me."

Avoiders are parents, like Tom and Ann, who are too preoccupied with their own affairs to share much time with their children. Or they may simply be parents who do not value sports; they may spend time with their children in other areas. They may be single parents who are burdened with having too many responsibilities to take on more.

There are advantages to this type of parenting, however. The child will probably not be subjected to excessive parental pressure. The child may develop a charming spontaneity and be very fun-loving. He or she may not develop a goal-directedness, however, that will help in other areas of life such as academic performance and career aspirations.

The Enabler

The Enabler does not make choices for the child but *enables* him or her to be successful in whatever direction the child chooses by giving support and positive encouragement. The parent will stress balance and give the child room to make personal decisions and choices.

The Enabler will help the child accomplish a goal, but not pressure the child at an early age to specialize. In athletics the Enabler will permit the child to experiment with various sports and enjoy learning them. Whether the child chooses to excel in sports or in other areas, the Enabler will support that child's decision.

Enablers believe in the development of the whole child, and believe in keeping a balance in the child's life between fun, skills development, and goal attainment.

As is evident in figure 1.4, the Enabler's profile shows balance. The level of involvement is often high, but the Enabler believes that a child

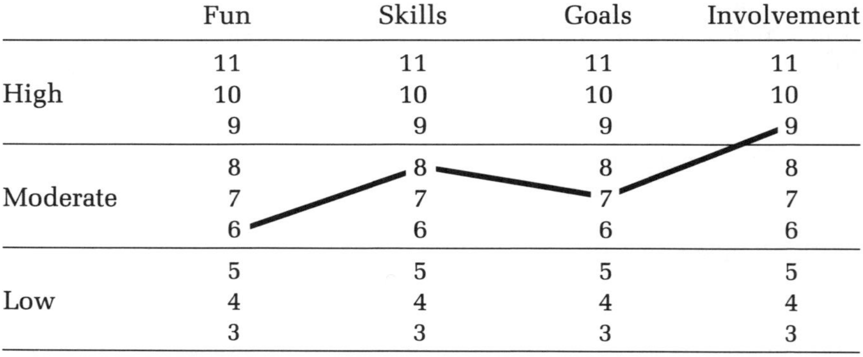

	Fun	Skills	Goals	Involvement
	11	11	11	11
High	10	10	10	10
	9	9	9	9
	8	8	8	8
Moderate	7	7	7	7
	6	6	6	6
	5	5	5	5
Low	4	4	4	4
	3	3	3	3

Figure 1.4 Profile of an Enabler.

should enjoy sports as well as learn skills and accomplish goals.

What follows is an account (Armstrong 1986) of one Enabler's approach to parenting.

Parenting the Elite Athlete

Hugh Armstrong is a psychologist in the faculty at the University of Washington. He and his wife Dolly are the parents of two exceptional athletes, Debby and Olin. Debby and Olin are both ski racers. Debby won the gold medal in the giant slalom at Sarajevo in 1984. Olin is a high-ranking junior racer.

The Armstrongs have always been an active family. They have spent time together swimming, hiking, bicycling, skiing, and traveling. Debby and Olin have never been pushed to be ski racers, even though Hugh and Dolly are weekend ski instructors at a nearby ski resort.

Throughout high school Debby was encouraged to participate in many sports. She starred in basketball, field hockey, and soccer. She was also a ski racer but was never encouraged by her parents to make that her only athletic goal. When Debby was twelve years old (a formative period for ski racers) the Armstrongs spent a year in a Far Eastern country while Hugh was on a sabbatical. They could have spent the year near a ski resort but did not. Hugh and Dolly take a balanced approach to parenting, which does not always include skiing in their children's development.

Hugh believes that the year in a foreign country helped give Debby a sense of independence, which has helped her in ski racing. "When you're in the starting gate you are all alone," Debby has said. Perhaps her year abroad helped her cope with having to rely on her own inner resources.

Hugh and Dolly believe that every child has the potential to be excellent in something, and it is the parents' job to help the child discover what that area of excellence is and then support it. "Don't demand excellence in a given field," says Hugh. "Remember, your child is excellent; just look for the ways in which that excellence displays itself" (Armstrong 1986, p. 9).

HOW THIS BOOK CAN BE HELPFUL TO YOU

The authors of this book believe that the Enabler role is the best type of parenting style for athletic children. The Enabler provides balanced parenting that allows room for the child to grow in his or her own way, but not without firm guidance and support.

If you are already an Enabler, your child is very fortunate. You will be a good guide in his or her development. You will also enjoy reading this book. It will give you much information and support for the attitude you have.

If you have determined that you are either a Persuader or an Avoider, this book can help you examine, and possibly change, your style of parenting.

If your profile is clearly that of a Persuader, the risk is that you might pressure your child too much. Your son or daughter might not be having enough fun in youth sports and may lose interest, quit, or burn out. You will benefit from reading the entire book carefully, but especially chapters 3 (sections on competitive stress) and 4 (steps on defining success and motivating your child).

For the Avoiders reading this book, you have already taken a step toward changing your parenting style. Congratulations! In general, you need to get more involved with your child. He or she needs your support, time, and guidance to become a successful athlete. You, too, will benefit from reading the entire book, but especially chapters 3 (section on how much time and money to spend) and 4 (note steps 1, 2, 3, 6, and 7).

Enjoy the journey you are about to take to the Enabler's circle. This is the place on the sidelines where you and your young athlete will feel intimacy and warmth. Be glad you have taken the time to examine yourself and to learn what positive parenting can do for your child.

REFERENCES

Armstrong, Hubert, "Parenting the Elite Athlete." *Puget Soundings* (February 1986), pp. 6–9.

Bloom, B. *Developing Talent in Young People.* New York: Ballantine, 1985.

Friedman, Jack. "Building the Perfect Player." *People,* 8 December 1986, pp. 59–63.

Hellstedt, Jon. "Family Characteristics of Ski Racers." Unpublished paper, 1986.

Smoll, Frank, and Ronald Smith. *Psychological Perspectives in Youth Sport.* Washington, D.C.: Hemisphere, 1977.

Chapter 2

Evaluating Sports Skills

by David G.A. Watson, M.D.

Parents and parents who coach like to know how to evaluate athletic skills in children. In recent years a number of testing programs have been developed to analyze and define certain physical skills. Many of these tests are technically sophisticated and can be performed only in specialized clinics. However, it is possible for parents to gather basic and useful information at home about sports skills.

In this chapter we will go through a simple testing program that describes athletic strengths and weaknesses. This testing incorporates the principles of a pediatric neurological examination and sports testing done by physical educators. There will be tests to describe strength, speed, quickness, reaction time, body coordination, hand-eye coordination, and body proportions.

Standard tests currently exist that measure strength, speed, endurance, and flexibility. These established tests and norms from organizations such as the American Alliance for Health, Physical Education, Recreation, and Dance (AAHPERD) have been used nationwide to assess youth fitness. Many of the tests described in this chapter were given to Westford, Massachusetts, school children in a 1983 testing program. They are a combination of AAHPERD and other tests.

WHAT EVERY PARENT SHOULD KNOW ABOUT PUBERTY AND GROWTH

Puberty is one of the most important variables in the development of a young athlete. Early puberty will accelerate performance at middle (junior high) or early high school. Late development may negatively affect an athlete's self-confidence because he or she loses ground to his or her peers. Correct assessment using performance age is crucial in the turbulent emotional time from ten to seventeen years. Parents can help their young athletes understand the impact that physical development has on their athletic success. Physical maturation affects athletic performance.

What is *puberty?*

Puberty is the process of physical maturation that includes sexual development and muscle and skeletal growth. Many parents think of puberty as only sexual maturation. Puberty starts when a small center in the brain, the pineal gland, sends messages to the testes in boys and the ovaries in girls. These organs begin to secrete the appropriate sexual hormone—testosterone in boys, estrogen in girls. The result changes the young child to a fully mature adult.

Puberty takes place over a three- to five-year period. It begins at about ten and one-half years for girls and twelve years for boys. Puberty is associated with many psychological changes such as changes in mood and self-esteem. The increased production of sex hormones produces a rapid enlargement in body size due to growth of the bones, especially the long bones of the arms and legs. These hormones also cause an increase in size of the body's muscles and organs, such as the heart, lungs, liver, and kidneys.

There are specific differences between boys and girls during puberty. For girls the increase in body fat is primarily around the hips, breasts, and thighs. The pelvis enlarges, and body hair develops. Menstruation usually starts two years after the beginning of puberty. For boys, shoulders broaden and the larnyx or voice box enlarges, causing the voice to deepen. Hair begins to grow on the face, and the penis and testicles enlarge.

After puberty males average five inches taller and fifty pounds heavier than females. After puberty males will usually have less body fat and more muscle than females.

When does puberty start?

It varies from child to child, and between boys and girls. On the average girls usually begin puberty at about ten and one-half years and boys begin puberty at about twelve years. The range is eight to fifteen years for girls, and ten to seventeen years for boys. Those girls actively involved in sports such as gymnastics may delay the beginning of menstruation until they are fifteen years old or older.

What does puberty have to do with athletic performance?

Puberty increases body size. More important, puberty increases muscle size in both boys and girls. This rapid increase in muscle size results in dramatic improvements in strength, speed, and endurance. For this reason, sports requiring these skills are easier to perform when athletes are more physically developed. An athlete who enters puberty late will be at a temporary disadvantage with his or her age group.

Puberty causes its changes over three and one-half years for girls and five years for boys. The start of puberty, rather than chronological age, should be a reference point when comparing strength, speed, endurance, and flexibility of young athletes.

How can I recognize the onset of puberty?

There are two ways in which to recognize the onset of puberty: by standard method and by self-assessment. By the standard method, for girls, the most obvious onset of puberty is breast development, although this test is not perfectly accurate (see figure 2.1). The beginning of puberty for boys, usually verified by a doctor's exam, is seen in the enlargement of the testicles (see figure 2.2). The appearances of facial and body hair and acne are less reliable but more obvious signs.

Many professionals have used a technique called self-assessment to recognize the onset of puberty. Children are given pictures of males or females in various stages of development, and are then asked to rate their own stage of development from these pictures. (For more information on the topic of puberty or stages of your child's development, ask your child's doctor.)

How do you determine pubertal age?

An alternative method of determining pubertal age, which we will call performance age, can be calculated by adding the average age of onset of puberty (*fixed* at ten and a half years for girls and twelve years for boys) to the number of years *since* your child's puberty actually started. Say, for example, a thirteen-year-old boy started puberty at ten years, three years ago. To calculate his performance age you would add three to twelve. In the case of a twelve-year-old girl who has *not* started puberty, you would add zero to ten and one-half. The reason for determining performance age is to understand a child's athletic ability in relation to his or her own physical maturation.

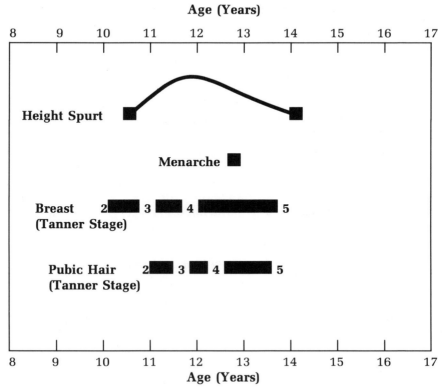

Source: Ross Laboratories, 625 Cleveland Avenue, Columbus, Ohio 43215.

Figure 2.1 Sequence of pubertal events: average American female.

Now I know my child's performance age, but how will it help?

By using the formula for performance age, you can compare his or her success in the tests of speed, strength, and endurance with that of other athletes at the same stage of development.

What about the older child, say, thirteen or fourteen years old, who shows no signs of puberty?

Children who develop puberty late, who do not suffer from malnutrition, usually are late bloomers. They grow later and longer and do not reach their full potential until late adolescence, or even into their twen-

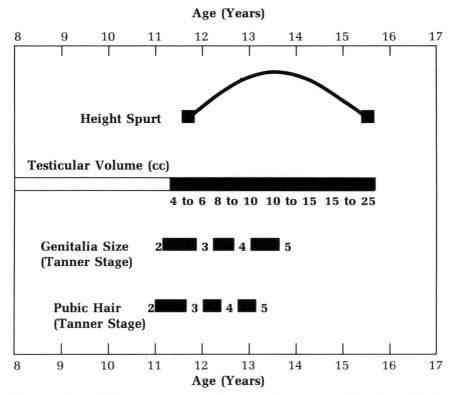

Source: Ross Laboratories, 625 Cleveland Avenue, Columbus, Ohio 43215.

Figure 2.2   Sequence of pubertal events: average American male.

ties. Their performance age remains ten and one-half for girls or twelve for boys until puberty starts. For example, a thirteen-year-old girl who shows no signs of puberty should have a performance age of ten and one-half years. Often these late bloomers turn out to be competent athletes later on.

What are the physical capability differences in sports skills between my child, who is a slow developer, and others his age who are more developed?

Figure 2.3 shows the growth change of three children from infancy to full adult. Notice that there are three lines. There is a line showing an average developer, an early developer, and a late developer. All of

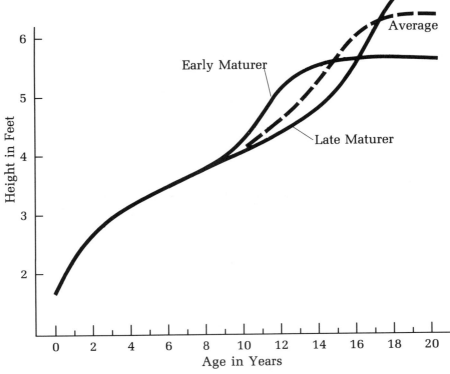

Adapted from pediatric records by David Watson.

Figure 2.3 Growth of three children from infancy to adult.

the children are about the same until seven or eight years of age. At this time the early developer begins to grow rapidly, far surpassing the other two. The early developer completes growth well before the other two have reached adult height. At about thirteen or fourteen years the late developer begins to fall behind the other two. However, by fifteen or sixteen years he or she is finally catching up and passes both the early and average developer, continuing to grow after the other two have finished. These growth patterns represent the different ways young athletes can develop.

Let's look at these three children at four times in their life. At six years of age all look the same in size, height, and weight.

At ten years of age the early developer is bigger, more muscular, stronger, quicker, and faster. The average developer and the late developer appear to be at the same stage of development. Neither has entered puberty.

At thirteen years of age the early developer is almost an adult. The average developer has shown some rapid growth, becoming stronger, taller, and more muscular, whereas the late developer still appears to be prepubertal. The late developer still has a preadolescent bone structure and musculature.

At twenty years of age all three have grown to be mature adults. The late developer, however, may be the tallest and the best athlete of the three, whereas the early developer, because of the early rapid growth and early maturation, is the shortest of the three.

In summation, an early developer shows early signs of athletic strength and speed. He or she will frequently have completed physical growth by fifteen. The average and slow developers will eventually catch up and often surpass the early developed superstars by becoming outstanding athletes in high school or college.

THE TESTS

Many times parents (and even the young athletes themselves) make comparisons between children and popular, world-recognized athletes. Successful world-class athletes, however, are abnormal (from Latin: *ab,* "away from," *norma,* "average"). It is their *abnormally good* performance of one or several skills that helps them succeed. Variables such as size, build, or flexibility obviously help athletes in some sports. Many basketball players are tall and have long arms. Rowers and high jumpers are usually taller than average. Gymnasts are generally smaller and more flexible. These characteristics are readily seen in the superstars. The average or good athlete need only be slightly better than normal to be recognized as successful in his or her sport.

It is possible to perform tests at home to learn about children's athletic capabilities. Very little equipment is needed, and the tests can be fun. One quick set of tests, however, will not give a complete picture of the child's total athletic potential. Used over a period of time the testing can be more helpful.

The tests that follow attempt to give a numerical value to the body's ability to coordinate, to balance, to sprint, to jump, to react. Scoring provides a general idea of the athlete's *raw* or *untrained* skill. Previous training, motivation, and body size may influence the results. Measurements should be taken before the child trains and can be used as a baseline to follow the child as he or she progresses throughout the program. Each test measures a slightly different skill and can apply to a different group of sports. Record individual test scores and other vital numerical data on the following test score sheet.

TEST SCORE SHEET

Name: _____

Birthdate: _____   Performance Age: _____

	Date Tested:	Score			
Physical					
Height:		___	___	___	___
Weight:		___	___	___	___
Sitting-standing height:		___	___	___	___
Arm span:		___	___	___	___
Flexibility:		___	___	___	___
Neurological					
Ruler drop:		___	___	___	___
Pegboard:		___	___	___	___
One-leg stand:		___	___	___	___
Hopscotch:		___	___	___	___
Dominant eye:		___	___	___	___
Muscles					
Vertical jump:		___	___	___	___
50-yard dash:		___	___	___	___
Chin-up:		___	___	___	___
600-yard dash:		___	___	___	___
One-mile run:		___	___	___	___

LEVEL 1: PHYSICAL EVALUATION

The following section examines anthropometric body proportions and includes tests of flexibility.

BODY PROPORTIONS

Measuring Height

To measure the athlete's height, ask him or her to stand against a wall with the back straight, feet flat on the floor, and eyes forward. To be sure you are getting the exact height, put your index finger under the jaw and lift upward gently so that the head is not tilted forward. It is best to use a flat, straight object for touching the top of the head. This object should form a right angle with the scale or wall where you are measuring. The measurement from the top of the head to the floor is called the standing height.

Measuring Weight

To measure weight accurately, use a balance scale if possible. The best time to measure weight is in the morning, before eating. The athlete should wear light indoor clothing without shoes.

Comparing Height and Weight

Using figures 2.4 and 2.5, find the point that represents the athlete's height and weight on the percentile curve at either the chronological age or the performance age point. The percentiles indicate your child's height and weight compared with those of other children of the same age and sex. A child at the fiftieth percentile is average, above the fiftieth percentile is taller and/or heavier than average, and below the fiftieth percentile is shorter and lighter than average.

A child in the higher percentile may be in a relatively higher percentile as an adult, though not always. Some young people grow for a longer period of time than others. On the average, the early developing child will usually stop growing earlier and grow to be a shorter and/or lighter adult.

During puberty, prediction of adult height and weight is difficult. The variable growth rates of children make predicting adult height or weight uncertain. If you use performance age, you can predict the variations in growth a little more accurately by standardizing the variations in growth. For example, a thirteen-year-old girl who has not begun puberty is on the tenth percentile. If you use her chronological age, her predicted height in the tenth percentile will be five foot one. By using her performance age (ten and one-half) and placing her in the fiftieth percentile, a more accurate prediction shows her adult height to be five foot four and one-half. This calculation takes into account her slower-starting growth period.

Measuring Body Fat

Caution should be taken in interpreting body fat by considering body weight. A child or athlete who has a body weight on a percentile greater than the body height is not necessarily overweight. He or she might have large bones and/or a large muscle mass. If someone measures much less on the weight percentile than on the height percentile, he or she is not necessarily underweight. That person may have a very slender body and small bones and muscles.

Accurate measurement of body fat is exceedingly difficult and usually requires the full facilities of a human performance or research laboratory.

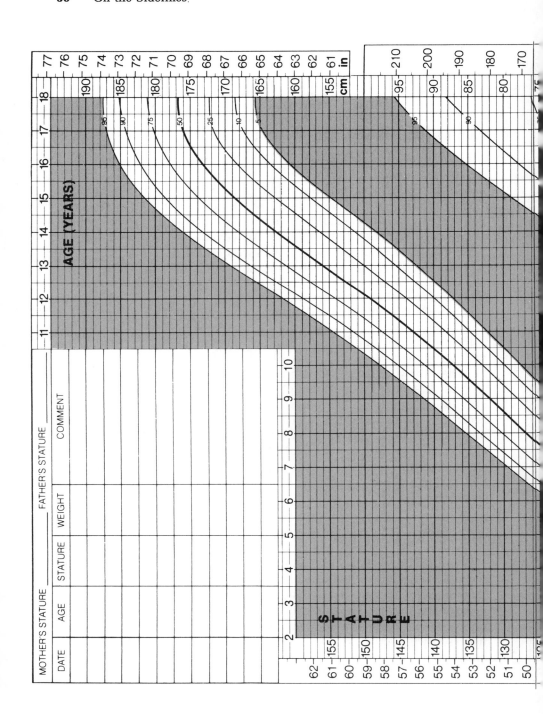

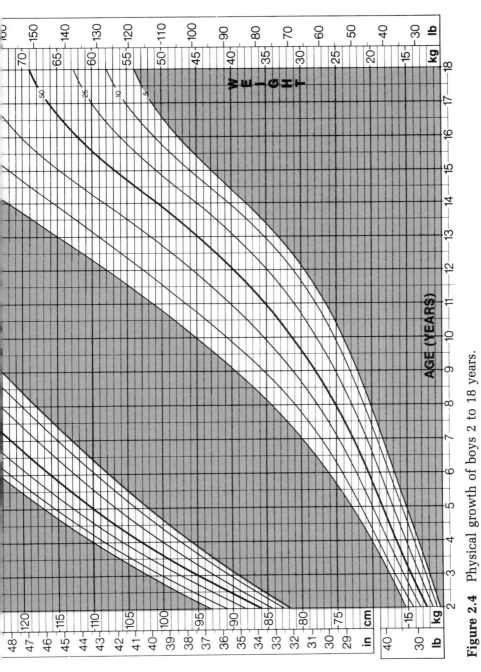

Figure 2.4 Physical growth of boys 2 to 18 years.

Source: National Center for Health Statistics (NCHS) percentiles.

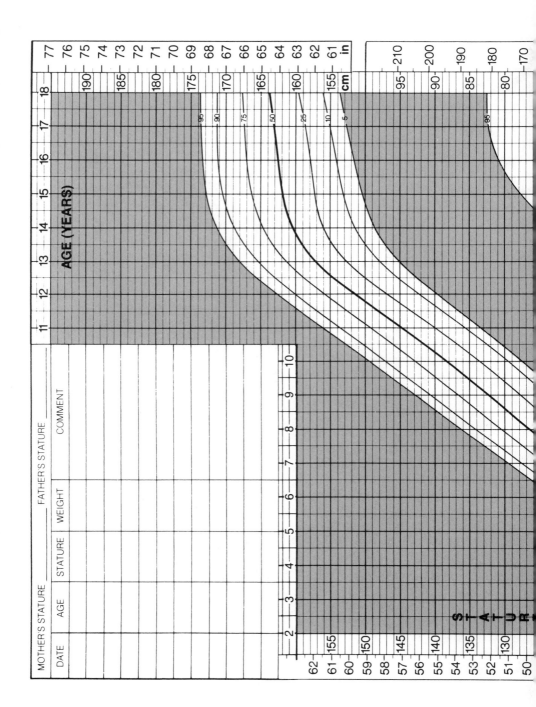

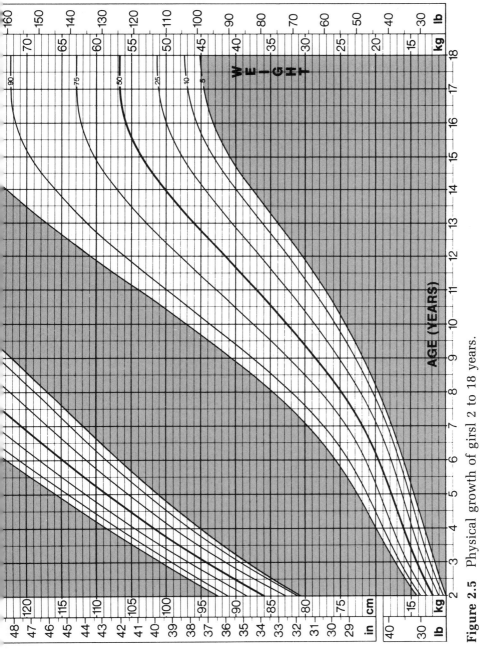

Figure 2.5 Physical growth of girsl 2 to 18 years.

Source: National Center for Health Statistics (NCHS) percentiles.

In these settings the most reliable method has been underwater weighing. Skin-fold calipers are reliable in expert hands but unreliable with untrained personnel.

Parents can perform a simple "pinch an inch" test. To do this test, gather a layer of fat and skin over the belly button, the thumb and forefinger separated by two inches, and pinch gently. People's fat deposition patterns differ and some may preferentially deposit fat in this area. It is reasonably safe to assume that an athlete with little or no subcutaneous fat over the abdomen is not overweight. It is not safe to assume, however, that this athlete is underweight.

Be very careful when making an assessment of body fat from weight measurements. Some athletes, particularly females in dance and figure-skating programs, become so obsessed with losing body weight that they become ill when attempting unrealistic weight reduction.

Measuring Standing-to-Sitting Height

Children's body proportions vary. Some have long legs, in relation to their shorter upper body; others have short legs. A convenient way to measure proportion (legs to body) is to measure the ratio of sitting and standing height. You have already measured standing height. Now measure sitting height.

The young athlete sits on the floor and a measurement is taken from the top of the head to the floor. This measurement is called the sitting height. Divide the sitting height into standing height. The ratio will tell you whether the upper or lower part of the body is relatively longer.

The example below shows the standing-to-sitting height for a certain five-foot-six athlete:

$$\frac{\text{Standing height} \quad 66 \text{ inches}}{\text{Sitting height} \quad 33 \text{ inches}} = 2.0 \text{ ratio}$$

Now plot this result against your athlete's age, using table 2.1.

Table 2.1   Leg and trunk length as a ratio of standing height to sitting height for boys and girls.

	Average Ratios According to Performance Age (Years)										
---	7	8	9	10	11	12	13	14	15	16	17
Boys	1.83	1.86	1.89	1.89	1.93	1.94	1.96	1.96	1.94	1.94	1.93
Girls	1.87	1.88	1.90	1.92	1.93	1.94	1.92	1.92	1.91	1.91	1.90

From Robert C. Cantu, M.D., *Clinical Sports Medicine* (New York: Macmillan, 1984), p. 9.

Table 2.1 indicates the average standing-to-sitting height ratio for boys and girls. Ratios above the average indicate legs longer than average for height, and ratios below the average indicate legs shorter than average (or trunk longer than average) for height.

In the case of a ten-year-old girl, for example, who is fifty-seven inches tall, weighs eighty-two pounds, and has a standing-to-sitting height ratio of 1.78, her height is below average because it is on the tenth percentile; her weight is average, or fiftieth percentile; and because the ratio is below fiftieth percentile, her trunk makes up a greater percentage of her body length than do the legs. This athlete is shorter and heavier than average and has shorter legs.

Measuring Arm Span

With arms outstretched, the measurement from fingertip to fingertip across the chest will describe arm span. The athlete's height is the best yardstick against which to measure arm span. An arm span longer than height indicates long arms, and an arm span shorter than height indicates relatively shorter arms. Long arms are useful for sports requiring reach and leverage, such as basketball and rowing.

Body Proportions and Sports

Height plays a major part in determining sports capabilities. Tallness for basketball is obvious. Jockeys are short, light athletes. Sports requiring a lot of balance and quick, coordinated movements are suited to smaller people. Most gymnasts are small.

Height is an advantage for high jumping and rowing. The longer body and limbs provide more leverage for the jumper on takeoff and for the rower on his or her oar strokes.

Short legs are an asset in balance sports such as skiing and skating, and in activities such as football blocking and running, in which the low center of gravity supports one's balance and strength. Long legs help the distance runner and cross-country skier, who rely on stride length and frequency to determine speed.

FLEXIBILITY

What is *flexibility*?

Flexibility is the pain-free range of movement of a joint (such as an ankle or knee) or group of joints (such as the back). This movement will be limited by the muscles and ligaments associated with the joint.

Ligaments are the fibrous strands that join the bones on either side of a joint. The movement of the wrist and thumb, for instance, is limited mainly by ligaments. The shoulder and hip, ball-and-socket-type joints, are held in place by both ligaments and large muscles surrounding the joints. Testing these joints will test not only the ligaments but the muscles around them. Shoulder movement is limited mainly by muscles. The hip joint and back are limited by ligaments and by the shape of the bones and hamstring muscles.

Because of the anatomical differences between joints, the amount of flexibility can differ greatly. Flexibility varies not only from person to person but from joint to joint in the same person. One athlete may have flexible hips and stiff wrists, whereas another athlete may have flexible joints in all parts of the body.

The following tests measure flexibility of the wrist, shoulder, and hip and hamstring muscles. Refer to figure 2.6 to score performance (1, less flexible; 2, average; 3, flexible), then total the scores for an overall flexibility score. Compare results with the overall performance scores in table 2.2. The higher the score, the more flexible the athlete.

Wrist and Thumb Test

Flex the wrist forward as far as it will go. Now grasp the thumb and try to touch it against the forearm. Not many people can do this exercise.

Shoulder Test

Reach down behind the neck with one hand. With the arm behind the back, bring the other hand up to meet it.

Hip Test

Stand with feet together and both knees straight. Bend forward at the waist and try to touch the toes. This test should be attempted only after a warm-up to loosen the hamstring muscles.

This test can be done more accurately using a sit-and-reach technique. Sit-and-reach means sitting with knees straight and reaching forward as far as possible. The feet should rest against a board that acts as an end point. If the toes can not be reached, the score is low. Greater flexibility is indicated by the number of inches that are reached beyond the toes.

Flexibility is often equated with fitness. The more flexible a child is, the better physical condition he or she is in. This notion is not always true, however. Flexibility is a component carried genetically. Differences

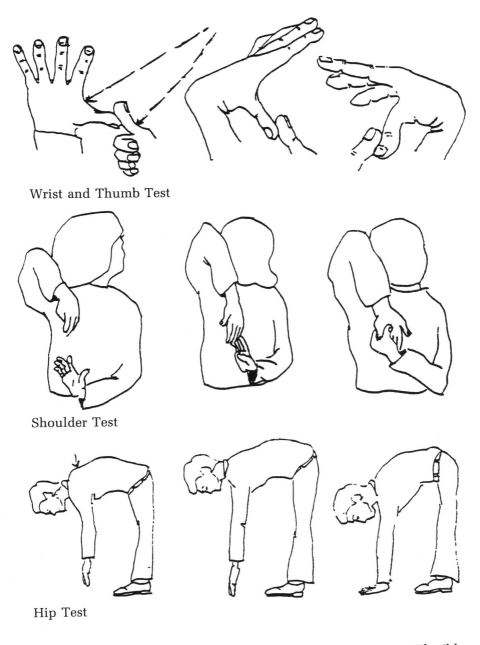

Wrist and Thumb Test

Shoulder Test

Hip Test

Less Flexible   Average   Flexible

Figure 2.6 Three tests for flexibility.

in flexibility are noticeable even in infants. Most infants are very flexible when born and lose some of that flexibility by five or six years of age. By puberty girls outpace boys in flexibility performance, as table 2.2 shows.

Table 2.2   Flexibility performance scores for boys and girls.

| | Average Combined Score From Three Flexibility Tests According to Performance Age | | | |
	9–10	11–12	13–14	15–16
Boys	6.0	6.0	5.5	5.0
Girls	6.0	5.6	6.7	7.0

From Robert C. Cantu, M.D., *Clinical Sports Medicine* (New York: Macmillan, 1984), p. 10.

Flexibility and Sports

Flexibility measurements have been applied in many sports. Dancers and gymnasts have a higher level of flexibility. Another very flexible group of athletes is swimmers, probably because good flexibility in the shoulder is helpful to the swimming strokes. According to world champion hurdler Renaldo Neamiah, flexibility is important for hurdling.

This testing is intended as a simple assessment and does not define precisely the flexibility of individual joints, ligaments, or muscles. It provides parents with a basic understanding of flexibility. A parent can help improve his or her child's flexibility by assisting in stretching programs. (See chapter 6 for a detailed flexibility program.)

LEVEL 2: NEUROLOGICAL EVALUATION

When a pediatrician tests a child's nervous system, several skills are tested. The child is tested for balance when standing upright and for fine motor coordination (the ability to make quick, repetitive movements with changes in direction). Gross motor coordination is evaluated by the child's ability to move his or her body, to turn, to jump, and to hop.

The following series of tests is designed to allow parents to make a similar type of assessment of balance and gross motor and body coordination that the doctor makes in the office. An additional test for reaction time, which is not usually part of the routine physical exam, has been added.

When talking about athletes, a coach will often describe one as having speed and another as being well coordinated or skillful. Larry Bird, for example, a Boston Celtics basketball player, can not run as fast or jump as high as other professional basketball players, yet he is unquestionably one of the best basketball players of all times. Why? Larry Bird is extremely well coordinated. His ability to make baskets consistently from all angles and all distances testifies to that.

In this section five tests will be used: the ruler drop, pegboard, one-leg stand, hopscotch, and the dominant eye. Each tests a different function of the brain and nerves.

REACTION TIME

What is *reaction time?*

When the eye sees, the hand feels, or the ear hears, the athlete reacts. The faster he or she reacts, the faster the brain is deciding on an action and moving the right muscles (the quicker the brain processes and sends out the nerve impulses, the faster the reaction time). The time taken to react to a stimulus is the time it takes the nerve impulse from the eye or finger to reach the brain, be processed, and be sent out via nerve pathways to the muscles, which finally move.

The Ruler Drop Test

There are several ways to test reaction time. The ruler drop test is the simplest and easiest test to perform.

To do the test, you will need a twelve-inch ruler (or twenty-four-inch ruler for children under ten). Hold it suspended vertically from the twelve-inch (or twenty-four-inch) end. Standing behind the seated child, hold the ruler vertically such that the zero end of the ruler is seen at eye level. The child spreads his or her fingers and thumb, with one inch between the thumb and index finger. The ruler's zero point is suspended midway between the finger and thumb. The child focuses attention on the ruler. The ruler is dropped without warning. The child is instructed to catch the ruler, as soon as it falls, between the finger and the thumb. Measure the point on the ruler at the top of the thumb. See figure 2.7.

Repeat the test until three consistent catches are made (within one-half inch). Table 2.3 records the average catch in inches for children seven to sixteen years of age.

The faster a child reacts, the shorter the reaction time. Someone with short reaction time is typically referred to as having quick reflexes or quick reaction. His or her brain quickly processes the signals it receives and sends out a coordinated message to take action.

Figure 2.7 The ruler drop test.

 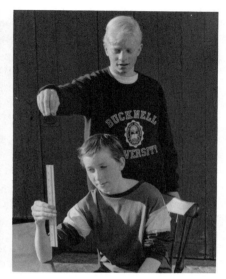

Table 2.3 Ruler drop performance scores for boys and girls.

	Score (inches) According to Chronological Age				
	7–8	9–10	11–12	13–14	15–16
Boys					
High	8.0	5.0	4.0	5.0	5.0
Average	10.0	9.5	6.5	7.5	6.0
Low	24.0	14.0	10.0	10.0	8.0
Girls					
High	11.0	6.0	4.0	5.0	5.0
Average	18.0	10.0	7.0	6.5	6.0
Low	24.0	14.0	10.0	10.0	8.0

From Robert C. Cantu, M.D., *Clinical Sports Medicine* (New York: Macmillan, 1984), p. 7.

Quick Reflexes and Sports

In several sports a faster reaction time is an asset. Measurements of elite athletes in tennis and baseball indicate that they have exceptionally good reaction times, although the advantage has not been universally established. Quick reaction time is helpful for goalies in sports such as lacrosse, ice hockey, and field hockey, and for cricket and squash players and race drivers. Reaction time is probably made up of several factors, in addition to fast response of the nervous system and an ability to focus attention.

HAND-EYE COORDINATION

What is *hand-eye coordination?*

During a pediatrician's neurological exam, the doctor sometimes asks your child to tap the back of his or her hand, or to touch his or her finger back and forth to the nose as rapidly as possible. The doctor is testing fine motor coordination, in this case hand-eye coordination, that is, the child's ability to make quick, controlled movements.

The Pegboard Test

The pegboard test uses coordination of the hands and eyes to move pegs back and forth between a series of holes drilled in a board. The emphasis is on quick, controlled movements of the hands and shoulder. For the child to perform this test well, the hands must move smoothly and quickly while moving the pegs. The shorter the amount of time it takes to do the test, the better the score.

First, you will need to make a pegboard. Take a board measuring twelve-by-twenty-four inches and drill three-quarter-inch holes in two rows, ten holes to a row. The rows should be eighteen inches apart and the holes one inch apart. To make the pegs you will need five-eighths-inch dowels. Make ten three-inch pegs. Place the pegs in one row. See figure 2.8.

Figure 2.8   The pegboard test.

The object of the test is to move the pegs, using the writing hand, one peg at a time, to the other side of the board and then back to the starting position. The athlete being tested is allowed one practice run. The test is timed.

Table 2.4 shows the average performance scores of children aged six through sixteen. Scores with lower time, of course, come with advancing age. Scoring well on this test at any age, however, means that the young athlete has good hand-eye coordination and should perform well in sports such as tennis, table tennis, and squash.

Table 2.4 Pegboard performance scores for boys and girls.

Age	6	7	8	9	10	11	12	13	14	15	16
Average score (seconds)	36	34	31	28	27	26	25	24	23	23	23

Data compiled by David Watson from testing program in Westford, Massachusetts, schools.

Hand-Eye Coordination and Sports

Quick, coordinated movements of the hands improve with age. Of course, at the same age, some people will be better than others. By about ten years of age, one's hand-eye coordinated movements do not improve, indicating perhaps that the brain and nerves have matured. Good hand-eye coordination is helpful for the following sports: tennis and table tennis, squash, golf, baseball, cricket, and fencing.

Hand-eye coordination can be improved with practice. By repeating a movement many times, the nerve pathways become facilitated (messages pass more easily along these particular nerve pathways). This improvement, however, applies only to the practiced movement and very similar movements. Practicing a tennis forehand, for example, will not improve a golf swing, but might help a racketball shot.

COORDINATION AND BALANCE

What are *coordination* and *balance?*

Coordination is the demand made on different parts of the body to perform a common action or movement. Balance is the physical equilibrium before or returned to after a motion or series of motions that upsets the normal weight distribution of the body.

The ability to maintain the body in a balanced, upright position depends on messages sent to the brain. These messages come from the ears, the muscles, the eyes, and the joints. They make the body aware of the body's positions, allowing adjustments to muscle tone to keep a balanced, upright position.

The following two tests measure motor coordination (the coordination of balance and large muscle groups), which controls the way an athlete runs, jumps, and, in fact, performs all actions using large muscle groups such as legs, arms, and back. Balance is tested first.

The One-Leg Stand Test

The young athlete is asked to stand on his or her leg, the dominant leg (the one he or she uses to kick a ball). The other leg is bent at ninety degrees at the knee. Once standing, the athlete is asked to close his or her eyes. The athlete should remain with hands at the sides with the support knee straight. See figure 2.9.

Figure 2.9   The one-leg stand test.

The time the athlete remains standing on one leg, with eyes closed, is the recorded score. Start timing as soon as eyes are closed. The time marked as finish is when the foot is moved, the raised foot touches the floor, or eyes are opened. If the young athlete remains balanced with eyes closed, the test is then terminated at thirty seconds. After thirty seconds, muscle fatigue becomes a factor and the youngster could be scored as having stood for an indefinite time.

Compare the athlete's time on this test with the average scores in table 2.5. The longer the athlete maintains balance, the higher his or her score will be.

Table 2.5   Balance test performance scores for boys and girls.

Age	6–7	8–9	10–11	12–13	14–15	16–17
Average Score (seconds)	4	13	12	18	20	20

Data compiled by David Watson from testing program in Westford, Massachusetts, schools.

Balance and Sports

This test integrates several systems: the balance organ in the ear, nerve receptors in the muscles and joints to give position sense, the brain integrating all the messages, and the muscles keeping the body in balance. Good balance is one aspect of overall coordination that is required in many sports, such as gymnastics, figure skating, springboard and platform diving, ice hockey, and downhill skiing.

The Hopscotch Test

Draw a hopscotch course for this test. Use an 8½″ × 11″ sheet of paper to mark block. Refer to figure 2.10. At your command the young athlete begins hopping. The child hops into the course with the left foot into box A and the right into box B, then hops on one foot into box C, then hops into D and E with left and right foot, one foot into F, two feet into G and H, and one foot into I, then turns around in that box and returns by the same method.

The test is timed. Use a stopwatch, timing from the moment the child jumps into the course and jumps out. Compare the results with the scores of other children as presented in table 2.6.

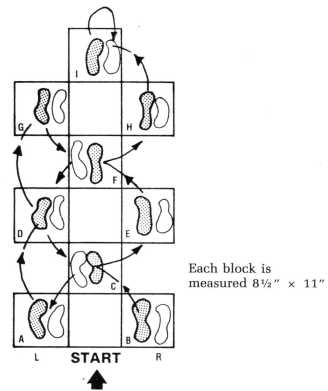

Each block is
measured 8½″ × 11″

Figure 2.10 The hopscotch test.

Table 2.6 Hopscotch performance scores for boys and girls.

	Score (seconds) According to Chronological Age				
	7–8	9–10	11–12	13–14	15–16
Boys					
High	6.0	4.5	4.2	4.4	4.4
Average	6.7	5.4	5.0	5.3	5.2
Low	7.5	6.0	5.7	7.0	7.0
Girls					
High	5.5	4.1	3.5	3.5	3.5
Average	6.2	4.8	3.9	4.0	4.7
Low	7.5	6.5	5.2	5.4	5.5

From Robert C. Cantu, M.D., *Clinical Sports Medicine* (New York: Macmillan, 1984), p. 7.

Coordination and Sports

Motor skill, as measured by the hopscotch test, depends on nerve control of muscles, as well as visual messages and messages from the balance organ in the ear. All these signals feed into the brain, and the brain coordinates the messages and programs muscle movements. The result is smooth, coordinated action.

Most sports rely on balance and body control. Sports demanding extremely fine-tuned motor coordination include skiing (alpine), gymnastics, springboard and platform diving, skating (figure and ice hockey), basketball, soccer and other field-team sports, golf, judo, and karate.

VISUAL ACUITY

Dominant Eye Test

We all use our eyes, but one eye dominates. Testing to find the dominant eye is simple. Use a cardboard tube, such as found in a roll of paper towels. Hold the tube horizontally at arm's length. With both eyes open, look down the tube and pick an object in the distance and fix that object in the tube. Close one eye and then the other. The object will be seen *through* the tube by only one eye. This is your dominant eye.

The results of this test (which have no numerical scoring value, of course) indicate that the dominant eye will fix on and track objects, such as a tennis ball or baseball, a little more easily than will the nondominant eye. Most professional baseball players are *cross-dominant* between hand and eyes, that is, right-handed batters are left eye dominant and left-handed batters are right eye dominant. The baseball player can benefit by knowing that the right-handed batter should stand such that the left eye is toward the pitcher. The left eye is then in a slightly better position to pick up and track the baseball as it is thrown. If the right eye is dominant, it will not be as easy to pick up and track the baseball in this position.

Of course, many professional baseball players are right-handed with right eye dominance, so this theoretical disadvantage can be overcome. It does seem to be an advantage for baseball players to be cross-dominant between one hand and their dominant eye.

LEVEL 3: MUSCLE EVALUATION

The following section examines muscle power and includes tests of speed or acceleration, sustained speed, and endurance.

MUSCLE POWER

What is *muscle power?*

There are three types of muscle power: explosive, short term, and long term. Sprinters use explosive power, middle-distance runners and swimmers use short-term power, and cross-country skiers and long-distance runners use long-term power. Different sports, therefore, appear to need specific types of muscle power. The series of tests in this section will help you identify the levels of each type of power your child demonstrates.

Training for a particular sport should be aimed at developing the type of muscle power specific for that sport. A sprinter, for example, needs explosive power, which is supplied by high-energy storage particles called *organic-phosphate molecules.* These particles are needed for one-hundred- and eight-hundred-meter sprints to strengthen the anaerobic energy system. *Anaerobic* means that oxygen is not necessary for the muscles to burn the fuel for energy. In anaerobics, starch or carbohydrates called glycogen, which is stored in the liver and muscles, are used to supply the muscles with fuel to burn. The long-distance athlete trains the aerobic system, which supplies prolonged energy by using oxygen to burn mostly fat as the muscles' fuel.

How does a muscle work?

The brain sends a message via the spinal cord and nerve to tell a muscle to contract. A muscle, which is made up of thousands of fibers, receives the nerve's message, telling it how many fibers should contract at one time and in what sequence.

Muscles burn fuel to supply the energy used for muscle contraction. A muscle is like the steam engine of a locomotive. Wood is added to the engine to increase the size of the flame, producing more heat and steam. When the locomotive climbs a steep hill, a large amount of fuel is placed in the fire to make it burn its hottest. This high level of heat lasts only a short time. On gradual slopes the wood is added slowly to maintain a moderate heat level. This level of heat lasts a longer time. When the locomotive cruises along a flat surface, the heat level does not have to be as high as when climbing hills. The lower heat level must be maintained to propel the locomotive forward. In order for the locomotive to make best use of the fuel supply, wood is added in small amounts over an extended period of time.

Muscles utilize three primary sources of energy while performing physical activities:

Type I (Adenosine Triphosphate [ATP]—Creatine Phosphate [CP]). Explosive power is supplied by energy storage molecules in the muscles called organic phosphates. Like the amount of fuel needed to propel the locomotive up a steep hill, this power source supplies energy for only a short period of time. During maximum muscle effort this fuel source provides optimal energy for approximately ten seconds.

Type II (Anaerobic Energy System). Anaerobic energy provides short-term speed when an activity lasts between thirty seconds and three minutes. Like the demand on fuel needed to propel the locomotive up a gradual slope, the prolonged and increased demand for energy in this system is supplied gradually over a period of time. The muscle utilizes the sugar in the blood and the sugar stored in the muscle as glycogen. During anaerobic exercise sugar is burned without oxygen to produce energy.

Type III (Aerobic Energy System). When a muscle works at a moderate intensity for a period longer than three minutes, it utilizes sugar and fat as its primary fuel source. Like the demand on fuel needed to speed the locomotive along a flat terrain, the less intense but constant demand for energy in this system is supplied in smaller quantities over an extended period of time. Oxygen is required to burn sugar and fat, supplying energy to the muscle.

Are boys and girls different in muscle power?

Although the energy to make muscle contractions is the same for both boys and girls, boys will perform better on all these tests of muscle power because they have larger muscles. Boys usually have less body fat, which makes them stronger pound for pound as compared with girls.

Can we test for muscle types?

A maximal work effort can be sustained only for a few seconds. For longer and longer periods of time, less and less maximal muscle power can be used. Only twenty percent of maximal muscle effort can be continued for long periods.

In the following series of tests for muscle power, three tests—the fifty-yard dash, the six-hundred-yard run, and chin-ups—include data from the standardized AAPHERD testing. Two other AAPHERD tests, adapted for the purpose of making assessment simpler, have been added. The vertical jump test is used instead of the traditional standing broad jump, mainly because the latter requires more coordination than some children are capable of performing. A one-mile run is recommended instead of the usual two- to two-and-one-half-mile run (or ten-minute run for distance), since some children may not be able to complete the longer run.

Speed has different components: starting speed or acceleration, sustained speed, and endurance. Tests for each of the different power types are described below.

ACCELERATION

The Vertical Jump Test

A good test for acceleration and Type I explosive power is the vertical jump. Ask the young athlete to put some chalk on the tips of the fingers of one hand. Standing against a wall, both feet flat on the ground, he or she reaches as high up as possible and touches the wall, leaving a chalk mark. Then ask the young athlete to crouch down and jump straight up in the air, touching the wall with the chalked fingers as high up as possible. Repeat three times. Measure the distance between the highest mark made while standing and the highest mark made while jumping. This distance is the vertical jump score.

Figure 2.11 The vertical jump test.

Table 2.7 rates the average vertical jumps for boys and girls aged six through sixteen. The more physically mature a child is, the better he or she will perform.

Table 2.7 Vertical jump performance scores for boys and girls.

	Score (inches) According to Performance Age				
	7–8	9–10	11–12	13–14	15–16
Boys					
High	11	12	13	20	22
Average	8	10	11	15	15
Low	5	7	9	12	11
Girls					
High	10	11	12	13	17
Average	7	9	10	11	12
Low	4.5	7	8	8	8.5

From Robert C. Cantu, M.D., *Clinical Sports Medicine* (New York: Macmillan, 1984), p. 5.

Acceleration and Sports

A good vertical jump means that the athlete's muscles use more high-energy molecules and contract quickly and powerfully. The more muscular athletes will perform better because they have larger muscle masses that produce more power.

Unfortunately, when using high-energy molecules, the muscles quickly deplete the power supply and can only be counted on for a few seconds at a time. It requires several minutes to regenerate the energy stores.

Athletes scoring well on this test are suited to sports requiring quick, repetitive muscle contractions with rest periods between the action, such as football, basketball, sprints (track and field), weight lifting, karate, figure-skating jumps, and rugby (backs).

The Fifty-Yard Dash Test

The fifty-yard dash differs from the vertical jump in that the vertical jump measures a single maximum muscle contraction, whereas the dash measures maximal running effort over a short distance. The dash also measures Type I explosive power, but over five to ten seconds.

Figure 2.12   Athlete running.

For your child to perform the dash, find a level, safe running area. Measure fifty yards. Record the time with a stopwatch. It is best to run two or three children together to provide motivation for each runner. Compare the time of your child's test (by performance age) with the times of other children as shown in tables 2.8 and 2.9.

Table 2.8   Fifty-yard dash test scores for boys.

Percentile	Age							
	10	11	12	13	14	15	16	17
25th	8.8	8.5	8.3	7.6	7.6	7.2	7.0	7.0
50th	8.2	8.0	7.8	7.5	7.1	6.9	6.7	6.6
75th	7.6	7.6	7.3	7.0	6.8	6.5	6.3	6.3
95th	7.0	7.0	6.8	6.5	6.3	6.1	6.0	6.0

Source: American Alliance for Health, Physical Education, Recreation, and Dance, 1900 Association Drive, Reston, Virginia 22091.

Speed and Sports

The fifty-yard dash test measures maximum sprinting speed. Sports in which such speed is an advantage include track and field (sprints), weight lifting, tennis, squash, and baseball.

Table 2.9 Fifty-yard dash test scores for girls.

Percentile	Age							
	10	11	12	13	14	15	16	17
25th	9.0	9.0	8.9	8.8	8.9	8.8	9.0	9.0
50th	8.5	8.4	8.2	8.1	8.0	8.1	8.3	8.2
75th	7.9	7.9	7.8	7.7	7.6	7.7	7.7	7.8
95th	7.0	7.0	7.0	7.0	7.0	7.1	7.0	7.1

Source: American Alliance for Health, Physical Education, Recreation, and Dance, 1900 Association Drive, Reston, Virginia 22091.

POWER-TO-WEIGHT RATIO

What is *power-to-weight ratio?*

During maturation the young athlete usually gains weight. This weight is a result of an increase in muscle size and, to some degree, an increase in body fat. Muscle strength increases faster than weight, especially in boys. The chin-up or pull-up test is a useful measure of power-to-body-weight ratio. The chin-up exercise uses arm, back, and shoulder strength. Type I muscle power will improve performance in this test, as will weight training, using the arms. Girls do not perform well in this test because of their greater body fat and less muscular arms and shoulders.

The Chin-up Test

For your child to perform this test, you must provide a well-secured bar, reachable only by short jump or step support. The athlete should grasp the bar with palms facing toward the body. He or she hangs with arms straight. At your command the athlete pulls up until the chin is above the bar. The athlete then lowers himself or herself down to the starting position, still hanging. This completes one chin-up. The athlete continues until he or she can not complete another chin-up. Score the number of chin-ups completed.

The stronger the athlete is, compared with body weight, the more chin-ups he or she can do. Compare your child's test results with the scores of other children as presented in tables 2.10 and 2.11 (using the athlete's performance age).

Muscle Power and Sports

Sports requiring good chin-up performance include gymnastics and weight lifting.

Figure 2.13 The chin-up.

Table 2.10 Chin-up performance scores for boys and girls.

	Score According to Performance Age				
	7–8	9–10	11–12	13–14	15–16
Boys					
High	5	10	10	10	14
Average	1.5	3	3	4	6.5
Low	0	0	0	0	0
Girls					
High	5	10	8	3	10
Average	1.5	3	1	1	3
Low	0	0	0	0	0

From Robert C. Cantu, M.D., *Clinical Sports Medicine* (New York: Macmillan, 1984), p. 6.

Table 2.11   Pull-up test scores for boys.

Percentile				Age				
	10	11	12	13	14	15	16	17
25th	0	0	0	1	2	3	4	5
50th	2	2	2	3	5	6	7	8
75th	4	4	5	6	8	9	10	10
95th	8	8	9	10	12	13	14	16

Note: On this AAHPERD test the hands are held with palms facing away from the athlete. No similar test for girls administered.

Source: American Alliance for Health, Physical Education, Recreation, and Dance, 1900 Association Drive, Reston, Virginia 22091.

SUSTAINED SPEED

The Six-Hundred-Yard Run Test

Athletes in a sport that requires them to produce nearly maximal power for one, two, or three minutes at a time rely on an anaerobic energy system, or Type II power. The four-hundred-meter, eight-hundred-meter, and mile run at international level all fall within this time frame. There are several tests to measure Type II power. The test described here is one designed for younger athletes.

Find a level and safe surface or use the high school track for this test. Six hundred yards are measured. The athlete should be instructed to start at a moderate speed and to run the last three hundred yards as hard as possible. Record the time by stopwatch.

Compare the time of your child's run (using performance age) with those of other children as shown in tables 2.12 and 2.13. The more physically mature a child is, the better he or she will perform.

Sustained Speed and Sports

A high score for this test means that the athlete uses sugar in his or her muscles efficiently and can sustain vigorous muscle activity. Muscles contract hard and long.

Training and excess body fat will affect this test. By running a lot of fast, short distances, such as in playing soccer or basketball, performance will improve. (For results unaffected by training, preseason testing will give a better baseline.) An overweight child can improve performance simply by shedding pounds and inches. Another factor improving per-

Table 2.12   Six-hundred-yard run test scores for boys.

| Percentile | Age | | | | | | | |
	10	11	12	13	14	15	16	17
25th	2:49	2:42	2:39	2:25	2:14	2:07	2:05	2:04
50th	2:33	2:27	2:21	2:10	2:01	1:54	1:51	1:50
75th	2:18	2:14	2:09	1:59	1:51	1:44	1:40	1:40
95th	1:58	1:59	1:52	1:46	1:37	1:26	1:24	1:23

Source: American Alliance for Health, Physical Education, Recreation, and Dance, 1900 Association Drive, Reston, Virginia 22091.

Table 2.13   Six-hundred-yard run test scores for girls.

| Percentile | Age | | | | | | | |
	10	11	12	13	14	15	16	17
25th	3:08	3:15	3:11	3:15	3:12	3:05	3:07	3:16
50th	2:48	2:49	2:49	2:52	2:46	2:46	2:49	2:51
75th	2:30	2:32	2:31	2:33	2:30	2:28	2:31	2:34
95th	2:05	2:13	2:14	2:12	2:09	2:09	2:10	2:11

Source: American Alliance for Health, Physical Education, Recreation, and Dance, 1900 Association Drive, Reston, Virginia 22091.

formance will be long legs. Long legs produce a longer stride to cover a greater distance.

Athletes scoring well on this Type II, anaerobic power test can do well in sports requiring frequent bursts of sustained speed, such as soccer and other field team sports, downhill skiing, speed and figure skating, swimming (sprints), and rowing. There will be some overlap with Type I and Type III power sources: short, fast bursts will use Type I power, and when the game slows down, Type III power will be used.

ENDURANCE

One-Mile Run Test

Running one, two, or three miles will test Type III aerobic power for all but well-trained athletes. Because training improves endurance so much, testing should be done on untrained youngsters, perhaps at the end of an off-season. The athlete should run a mile course over a level, paved surface or on a track. Advise him or her to start slowly and gradually, then to pick up speed, so that the last quarter is run the hardest. The athlete is timed using a stopwatch.

Using your child's performance age, compare his or her time with those of other children as presented in tables 2.14 and 2.15. The more physically mature a child is, the better he or she will perform.

Endurance and Sports

Cardiovascular conditioning (the increased efficiency of the heart, lungs, and circulation) plays an important part in the performance of Type II and Type III power. Training helps the heart and circulation (blood vessels) perform more efficiently. The heart enlarges and pumps more blood with each beat, which, as a result, means that more blood can be pumped during exercise. Small blood vessels called capillaries enlarge, making blood flow into the muscles more easily and more efficiently. The result is a quicker supply of oxygen and sugar (muscle fuel) to the muscles, enabling them to work harder and longer. To use this efficient power supply, muscle work must continue just below the level at which energy use outstrips supply. The faster the athlete can run or row or swim before reaching this level, called the anaerobic threshold, the better he or she will score in this test.

Athletes scoring well on the Type III, aerobic power test will usually not be fast starters. Often the slow starter or slow sprinter is better suited for endurance sports. Examples of sports using Type III aerobic power are distance running, cross-country skiing, distance swimming, and the triathlon.

FINDING THE RIGHT SPORTS

Sports can play an important part in a child's development and in the parent-child relationship. A child can experience joy, anger, sadness, and competitive pride and cooperation. Healthy participation in sports can prepare a young athlete for many of life's challenges.

What sports are my child best suited for?

Have your child complete all the tests in this chapter. Look at the results as a kind of athletic profile indicating physical strengths and weaknesses. You have learned how to measure speed, endurance, coordination, reaction time, and body proportions. You have compared your child's test results with the average scores of other children of the same age and sex.

Table 2.14 One-mile run test scores for boys.

Percentile	Age												
	5	6	7	8	9	10	11	12	13	14	15	16	17
25th	16:05	15:10	14:02	13:29	12:00	11:05	11:31	10:00	8:35	8:02	8:04	8:07	8:26
50th	13:46	12:29	11:25	11:00	9:56	9:19	9:06	8:20	7:27	7:10	7:14	7:11	7:25
75th	11:32	10:55	9:37	9:14	8:36	8:10	8:00	7:24	6:52	6:36	6:35	6:28	6:36
99th	7:45	8:15	7:17	6:14	6:43	6:25	6:04	5:40	5:44	5:36	5:44	5:40	5:41

Source: American Alliance for Health, Physical Education, Recreation, and Dance, 1900 Association Drive, Reston, Virginia 22091.

Table 2.15 One-mile run test scores for girls.

Percentile	Age												
	5	6	7	8	9	10	11	12	13	14	15	16	17
25th	17:59	15:27	14:30	14:16	13:18	12:54	12:10	11:35	10:56	11:43	12:21	13:00	11:28
50th	15:08	13:48	12:30	12:00	11:12	11:06	10:27	9:47	9:27	9:35	10:05	10:45	9:47
75th	13:09	11:24	10:55	10:35	9:58	9:30	9:12	8:36	8:18	8:13	8:42	9:00	9:03
99th	9:03	8:06	7:58	7:45	7:21	7:09	7:07	6:57	6:20	6:44	6:36	6:33	6:54

Source: American Alliance for Health, Physical Education, Recreation, and Dance, 1900 Association Drive, Reston, Virginia 22091.

Use these tests, first of all, to find strengths. A test may predict that the child has good explosive muscle strength, which can suggest certain sports that require that kind of skill. Looking for weaknesses should only be for established athletes in search of ways to strengthen deficiencies.

Use these tests to follow progress in performance. Follow gains in height, strength, speed, and reaction time, and compare these with the normal.

When is the best time to start my child in sports?

Sports requiring sharp reaction time and good hand-eye coordination can be introduced about seven to eight years of age. Sports requiring body balance, such as skiing and skating, can be introduced as early as five years of age. Sports requiring muscle power, such as football, should only be introduced to the fully mature athlete.

REFERENCES

American Alliance for Health, Physical Education, and Recreation. *Youth Fitness Test Manual.* Washington, D.C.: AAHPER, 1975.

American Alliance for Health, Physical Education, Recreation, and Dance. *Health Related Physical Fitness Test Manual.* Reston, Va.: AAHPERD, 1980.

Cantu, Robert C., M.D. *Clinical Sports Medicine.* New York: Macmillan, 1984.

GUIDE TO SPORTS SKILLS

Each athlete has a unique profile. Match your child's strengths with those listed in the following sports categories.

Bat and Racket Sports

These sports require fast reaction time and good hand-eye tracking, as well as excellent all-around vision:
Baseball, tennis, cricket, squash, racketball

Skill	High test score applicability
(in relative order of importance)	
—Quick reaction	Ruler drop
—Hand-eye coordination	Pegboard
—Speed	50-yard dash
	Vertical jump
—Cross-dominant hands and eye (baseball)	Dominant eye

Field-Game Sports

These sports require intermittent bursts of speed, body coordination, and, for some, hand-eye coordination:
Soccer, field hockey, lacrosse, rugby, basketball

Skill	High test score applicability
—Body coordination	Hopscotch
—Speed	50-yard dash
—Sustained speed	600-yard dash
—Hand-eye coordination (hockey, lacrosse)	Pegboard
—Tall, long arms (basketball)	Height and arm span

Endurance Sports

For these sports speed is often a disadvantage. Long legs and/or arms and endurance stamina are required:
Distance running, distance swimming, cross-country skiing

Skill	High test score applicability
—Endurance running	One-mile run
—Long legs	Sitting-standing height

Swimming Sports

Skill	High test score applicability
—Flexible	Flexibility test
—Long trunk	Sitting-standing height

Strength and Power Sports

These sports require short bursts of speed:
Football, track and field (throwing sports and sprints), weight lifting

Skill	High test score applicability
—Explosive muscles	Vertical jump
—Power-to-weight ratio	Chin-ups
—Speed	50-yard dash
—Acceleration	Vertical jump

Chapter 3

Children and Sports: Anticipating Your Questions

by Jon C. Hellstedt, Ph.D.

Sports as a form of play and recreation are beneficial for both children and adults. Exercise is good for mental health. It reduces anxiety and depression. Many positive habits are learned in youth sports participation that carry over into adult life.

Spontaneous backyard or informal sports are good for children. They are a form of play that provide healthy outlets for fun and physical exercise.

Organized sports programs, however, present a structure and a pressure that are absent in informal sports. As organized competitive sports have grown in popularity, psychologists have begun to study their effects on children. Questions have been raised about children, at increasingly younger ages, being placed in competitive situations where winning and losing are singular concerns. Are organized youth sports good for children? Should six- and seven-year-old children participate in games in which they are under pressure to win? Does the pressure to win, which often comes from adult coaches and parents, create stress that children are too young to handle?

Another area of concern to psychologists and parents alike is sport specialization. Many youth sports programs—hockey, soccer, gymnastics, skating, skiing—are highly competitive, and children are being pressured to specialize exclusively in one sport at an increasingly younger age.

As psychologists, physicians, and physical education practitioners study youth sports, some knowledge is developing that can help parents in deciding whether their children will benefit from organized youth sports. This chapter will summarize this knowledge by providing answers to some basic questions:

- Are youth sports good for children?
- Can youth sports be harmful to children?
- What are the causes of competitive stress?
- What can parents do to prevent competitive stress?
- What makes the difference between youth sports participation being beneficial and harmful for children?
- Why do children drop out of competitive sports?
- At what age should a child enter competition?
- At what age should a child specialize in one sport?
- How much time and money should parents spend on youth sports?
- Should I coach my own child?
- Are athletes born or made?

Are youth sports good for children?

The answer to this question, in the majority of cases, is yes.

Psychologists who have studied children in organized sports believe that the positive benefits of organized sports are in the following areas: fun, skills development, goal setting, self-concept development, coping skills, introduction to the competitive environment, and development of social and interpersonal skills.

Fun. The reason most frequently cited by children for participating in youth sports is to have fun. The joy of running fast, enduring a long run, flying through the air on a long jump, speeding down a ski slope, catching a softball or flying hockey puck—all are sensations young athletes experience in sports. Further, if children learn to be comfortable with speed, height, movement, and bodily contact when young, these sensations will enrich their adult recreational life.

Skills Development. When asked why they like to participate in sports, children often respond by saying that they like to develop new skills. They like to learn high-speed turns in skiing, jumping off bumps, hitting a baseball, shooting a basketball with accuracy, and doing flips in gymnastics or diving.

Goal Setting. Being successful in life is a process of learning how to set realistic goals and then achieving them. The young child playing basketball likes to be in the starting lineup or be the top scorer on the team. This desire helps the child to set goals to improve skills. Goal setting teaches many children the value of reaching beyond their present abilities.

Self-Concept Development. Youth sports can also teach a child a healthy sense of his or her limitations. There is always someone better, faster, or more skilled. Not everyone will make the first team. Though sometimes hard to accept, these lessons learned from sports help children develop a realistic perspective on their strengths and weaknesses.

Coping Skills. Sports provides a laboratory for learning to cope with emotions. In sports children can be spontaneous: they can yell, jump in the air with excitement, get angry, and feel sad, nervous, and tense. They can learn how to cope with anger and frustration. Young athletes learn to experience the excitement as well as cope with the fears that come with competition. These lessons learned will be useful when they face adult pressures.

Introduction to the Competitive Environment. We live in a competitive society. Schools are competitive. The pressure to get into many colleges is intense. Success in business or a professional career often depends on the young adult's desire to work hard to achieve goals. Youth sports introduce the child to competition. They can be a training ground for life in the real world.

Competition is almost innate with children. In spontaneous backyard (or street) games children will set up a scoring system and informal rules to govern play. They will select their teams by a careful selection system, and they will keep the team balanced to make the game highly competitive.

In organized youth sports the rules are more formal and the selection systems are controlled by adults, but the fun of competing remains. Many athletes, when asked why they participate in sports, say very simply, "I like to compete." They like to be able to measure their abilities by comparing themselves to others.

How does competition affect their personality development? There is some evidence from psychological research that athletes develop desirable character traits that help them in the adult world. Barry Smolev (1976), a psychiatrist, studied the personality traits of varsity athletes at UCLA and compared them with nonathletes. He found that the athletes showed more assertiveness and emotional expressiveness and had fewer symptoms of depression. Sport psychologists, such as Robert Rotella and Linda Bunker (1987), believe that young athletes develop self-discipline, time management skills, self-confidence, and the ability to work cooperatively with others.

Development of Social and Interpersonal Skills. Young athletes frequently say that they like to participate in sports because they can meet other children, form relationships, and spend time with their friends.

We all have a strong social need to feel included in a group. Through team sports children learn to work with others and to subordinate personal goals for the benefit of the group. This attitude can serve as a model and base for affiliations that will develop throughout life. Learning to be part of a team will help in adult life when group and interpersonal skills are required for negotiating in a corporate boardroom or in a project management group.

Social skills can develop in individual sports, too. Though they compete as individuals, young athletes get to know many other children through their training. For example, young gymnasts compete against each other as individuals, yet feel a sense of affiliation with the children from their team and from other programs.

Youth sports also give young children opportunities for relating to the opposite sex. This is especially true in adolescence, when participation and spectatorship at athletic events provide opportunities for heterosexual contact in a safe and nonthreatening setting.

Can youth sports be harmful to children?

The majority of children benefit from youth sports. They have fun, meet friends, and learn skills that will help them throughout life. Some children, however, have negative experiences in youth sports.

Organized youth sports require children to compete at early ages under the evaluative eye of parents and coaches. Winning and losing become important in many programs—sometimes too important. The children are asked to win or lose in the presence of their peers. They are subjected to negative criticism and pressure to perform.

Negative outcomes of youth sports mainly fall into three areas: development of low self-esteem, learning aggressive behavior, and development of excessive anxiety.

Development of Low Self-Esteem. Low self-esteem can result from the child's hearing and incorporating negative verbal and nonverbal messages. These can be communicated by parents, coaches, and peers.

Two psychologists from the University of Washington, Ronald Smith and Frank Smoll (1982), have studied the effects of youth sports coaches (in this case Little League baseball) on children. Though they did not find a direct relationship between coaches' use of criticism and low self-esteem, they did find that young athletes whose coaches used positive encouragement had higher self-esteem scores at the end of the season than did children who played for less supportive coaches.

Michael Passer (1984) summarizes studies of stress in youth sports participants and indicates that children worry about how their parents and coaches will evaluate their performance. They also worry about how their peers and teammates will evaluate their performance. These studies give empirical support for the many personal testimonies that have been provided in the media by those who have been emotionally harmed by youth sports experiences.

Only Nine and He Knows It

Robert Greene, in an article published in the *Boston Globe* (1981), describes the experience of a nine-year-old boy named Mark.

After waiting three years for the chance to play Little League baseball, Mark finally made the team. Mark was very excited and felt great about himself. Greene writes, "His parents took him to the first practice, and they could see it in his eyes: He idolized the man who was coaching the team. The other boys had played in years before—they start young—but Mark didn't care. At last he was going to be one of them."

Mark doesn't get to play much—one inning a game. As the season goes on he gets more disappointed. One evening, though, was particularly difficult for Mark. Only nine players show up for a game, so Mark is told he'll start in right field. His pride and excitement mount. But halfway through the first inning a regular shows up on his bike and the coach takes Mark out for the rest of the game.

Mark finishes the season, but his excitement is gone. His parents wonder, is it worth it? "All they know is that their son, at the age of nine, has been shown that he isn't good enough. The other night, Mark told his parents that he wasn't going to play baseball next summer. The eyes weren't as bright: that's what hurt his parents the most. The eyes weren't as bright."

What happened to Mark happens to many young boys and girls. Low self-esteem can result from not making the team, not getting adequate playing time, or suffering a humiliating experience. Many young boys and girls have ended a season feeling like Mark.

Low self-esteem can also result from not fulfilling parental expectations. Many children leave sports feeling incompetent because they could not please their parents. The young person is not able to achieve the parents' dream of being the best pitcher, goal scorer, skier, figure skater, gymnast, or tennis player.

I Never Pleased Him

A young man who is now a very successful manager in a high-tech manufacturing company, but who has always suffered from low self-esteem, looks back on his years in youth baseball and recalls the following: "My father was my coach. He always pressured me. He yelled at me when I struck out. He expected me to always throw strikes. If the team lost he would blame me. He never praised me when I did well."

Although this young man became a successful high school pitcher, and today is an excellent athlete (often shoots in the seven-

ties in golf and is a strong softball player on his town team), he has
had to struggle to overcome these childhood experiences. He maintains deep within the self-perception that he is not as good as others,
that he will be hurt by people if he gets too close to them. He is
apprehensive of being criticized by his bosses at work. To this day
he remains angry and emotionally cut off from his father.

Learning Aggressive Behavior. In sports there is a fine dividing line
between being appropriately assertive and being overly aggressive. Aggressive behavior is intended to hurt an opponent either physically or
psychologically, such as fighting or making an intentional disabling foul.
Assertive behavior, on the other hand, is using physical force to its maximum legal limits, such as making a hard but clean block in football.

Leaders in youth sports programs often fail to make this distinction.
Aggression and violence, though officially against the rules, are con-
doned by many sports organizations. A study of Canadian youth hockey players (Smith 1980) indicated that 58 percent of the participants at
the youngest level (nine- and ten-year-olds) approved of fighting even
though it was against league rules. This percentage increased to 84 percent among older youth hockey players! Here is clear evidence that some
sports teach children to condone and participate in aggressive behavior.

Critics of youth sports often attack the emphasis on winning that per-
vades many programs. Children are exposed to adult coaches and parents who yell at officials and fight over rule interpretations. In the
collision sports, such as football and hockey, they are told to hit hard
and be aggressive. In some cases they are taught to be violent.

Development of Excessive Anxiety. Some stress and anxiety are present in all sports. All athletes feel internal pressure and tension when
they enter competition.

Most young athletes like the challenge and excitement of competition. They use words to express this excitement like *psyched* or *pumped*.
And a certain amount of anxiety is a positive thing for children to experience. It is an internal state they will be exposed to throughout life.

Anxiety can also be a motivator. Studies show that successful athletes
often use a low to moderate level of anxiety as a motivator, a driving
force, to perform well. Sport psychologists call this motivator arousal.
The relationship between anxiety, arousal, and athletic performance is
demonstrated by the inverted U shown in figure 3.1.

As the arousal level increases, so does the athlete's performance
level—until it reaches a certain point. Then arousal is converted to fear
and nervousness, which interfere with athletic performance. The athlete may become distracted by internal pressures of wanting to win or

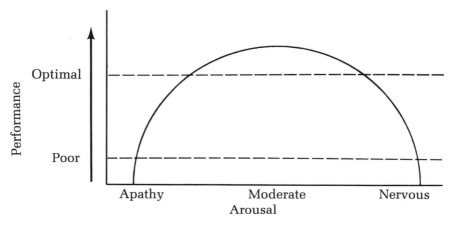

Figure 3.1   The relationship between arousal and athletic performance. *Source:* Bunker and Rotella (1977), p. 84.

external pressures such as the spectators or coach. The result can be mental errors and diminished performance.

The Inverted U in Action

An example of how the inverted U works can be shown in the case of a young basketball player, Chris.

As Chris arrives at the gym for the game that night, she is feeling somewhat flat emotionally. She isn't pumped up for the game. She feels listless as she gets dressed. If she were to go out and play in this emotional state, her performance level would be poor. Her performance would be at the lower left of the U-shaped curve in figure 3.1.

The coach gets the team together and tells them how important the game is that night. Chris begins to get aroused and feels more "with it." The team goes out for warm-ups and Chris feels her rhythm. She begins to get psyched. Her first-half play is excellent. She shoots well, rebounds effectively, and plays excellent defense. She is at the top portion of the curve.

Near the end of the third quarter, Chris begins to get nervous. The game is close; the opponent seems to be getting stronger as the game progresses. Her feeling of being psyched begins to change to a tenseness in her body. Her muscles feel tight. She begins to feel tired. She starts having thoughts like "We're going to lose." Chris begins to make a few errors. She creates a turnover. She tenses more. Her shots begin to miss the basket. Her concentration is broken. She passes the ball and it goes out of bounds.

Chris has moved to the righthand side of the curve. Her nervousness is creating performance errors. She needs to relax and regain her moderate amount of arousal to improve her performance.

Some young athletes have repeated experiences such as Chris did at the end of the game. They view competition as threatening or fearful. They worry that they will fail the team or be negatively evaluated by others. The result is an unpleasant inner feeling accompanied by muscular tension—what sport psychologists call competitive stress. The term *anxiety* is often used synonymously with stress, but actually refers to a more transient and temporary feeling. Anxiety is what any athlete feels as competition begins. Persistent or excessive anxiety develops into competitive stress.

What are the causes of competitive stress?

Competitive stress is a persistent fear of the competitive environment. A child with competitive stress might "choke" in competitive situations or avoid them altogether. It is caused by the child's having previous failure experiences, such as repeatedly striking out or falling during ski races. It can also result from exposure to negative evaluations of performance from coaches and parents, and to a lesser extent from peers. A third cause is injury and the fear of reinjury.

Tara Scanlan (1984), a psychologist who teaches at UCLA, has done extensive research on competitive stress in children. She has studied children in both individual (wrestling) and team (youth soccer) sports. She concludes that competitive stress occurs when the child perceives that the demands of the situation are greater than his or her abilities to meet them. In youth sports it typically occurs when a child believes he or she can not execute a skill well enough to receive favorable approval. An example might be a tennis player who is playing in a match against a player who is perceived to have better ability.

Competitive stress is not limited to athletics. It develops in the same way in academic, musical, artistic, or any other performance area. In fact, Scanlan states that research on performance anxiety indicates that solo musical performances generate more pre-event stress than sports performances.

An indication of competitive stress is the avoidance of or ambivalence toward participation in sports competition. If your child does not want to play in a tournament, it may be a sign that the child fears the competitive environment. Other signs would be agitation before games, not eating, or being quiet and withdrawn.

It is important to recognize early signs of competitive stress because if they are overlooked and the expectations to perform continue from coaches and parents, youth sports burnout may result. Burnout is caused by anxiety and stress building up to the point where the child becomes overwhelmed by the demands of the sport and has to escape from it in order to cope emotionally.

The following excerpt from an article by Davis Bushnell (1986) highlights the problems of burnout in young athletes.

Burnout

Tennis organizations are having to come to grips with an issue that is an inevitable byproduct of a sport which, at the professional level, is offering more prize money than ever before.

The issue is burnout, an aerospace term commonly used now to describe persons suffering from excessive stress, either mental or physical. Wherever a premium is placed on competition—whether it be in a business office or on a playing field—burnout is a problem.

Tennis fans have blamed burnout for the demise of the promising careers of Tracy Austin and Andrea Jeager, both halted by mental and physical woes. But tennis officials are increasingly aware of burnout cases involving juniors who have just begun to play competitive tennis regionally. The cause is the same: too much, too soon.

"Parents see the dollar signs, but they frequently lose sight of the astronomical odds against their kids ever turning pro," said [a former national tennis champion], who now plays only social tennis and works as a financial services consultant in Boston. "And parents are the controlling factor. They're the ones who choose the coaches and put their youngsters in certain programs."

"Parents may be easily blamed for being stress inducers and some deserve the blame, but the coaches role shouldn't be overlooked," said a teaching pro who requested anonymity. "I know that there are some teaching pros who are aggressively competing against each other for some of the most promising junior players in New England," he said. "What we need is a more centralized system so that these juniors can not only be taught skills, but also the right frame of mind."

"What is really needed is more direction from the ITF and the USTA," said Bill Floor, a teaching pro at Lincoln, Rhode Island's Fore Court III. The club has seven juniors who play national events. "I think the USTA should help us by not permitting kids twelve and under to play national tournaments. Youngsters pushed onto the national scene too soon end up with emotional and physical problems," Floor said.

Bill Drake, pro at The Country Club in Brookline who's noted for his work with circuit player Tim Mayotte, thinks the child should signal when he's had enough. And, most important, that decision must be respected. "Too many parents go past the supportive role, assuming the roles of their kids. That's why you'll hear parents say during a match, 'We're winning' or 'We're losing.'"

Young athletes who are in a state of burnout show many signs of agitation and depression. The signs of agitation include sleep disturbances, skin rashes, nausea, headaches, and muscular rigidity. Signs of depression might be lack of energy, appearing sad or unhappy, frequent illness, and a loss of interest in training and competing. It is important to watch for these signs, because during periods of depression athletes are more susceptible to injury. In this state of mind injury can become an acceptable way to exit from the pressure.

In addition to finding that competitive stress results from excessive pressure to win or excel, Michael Passer (1984) speculates that children with competitive stress have been raised in families where certain parental behaviors have prevailed. One of these is frequent negative performance appraisal. When the child performs in sports, the parents will be critical of the child's performance rather than supportive.

Second, the more intense the criticism, the more anxiety is likely to develop. In other words, the degree of parental anger or disapproval the child feels will increase the tendency toward being anxious.

A third parental practice that produces high anxiety is inconsistent feedback. If the parents say one thing (such as "Winning isn't everything") and then do another (such as get angry when the child loses), the child will get confused by the mixed messages.

Finally, parental overprotection or restrictiveness does not allow a child to be exposed to new and different situations. If parents are always there, hovering over the child, the child may not develop the necessary coping mechanisms. Without the ability and freedom to develop his or her own coping mechanisms, the child might panic in competition.

What can parents do to prevent competitive stress?

The answer to this question will be discussed in more detail in chapter 4. Briefly, however, there are some things parents can do to reduce stress in their children.

The main thing is to deemphasize winning and encourage individual skills development. A parent should positively reinforce improvement and effort. If a child learns to run faster, kick farther, or dribble better at the end than at the beginning of the season, he or she has accomplished a worthy goal.

Second, parents should take a positive approach. Praise your child for improved performance and for effort.

Third, parents should be sure there is a good match between the child's ability and the sport environment. Vying for the top team could be a mistake for a child who is not as skilled as the other children. A lower-level team would be better.

Parents must be careful to have realistic expectations and goals for the child. Few athletes become Olympic champions. Most participate in sports for enjoyment and fun, and get few external rewards such as fame, money, and athletic scholarships. Parents should not expect their children to be champions, but should teach them to work hard, set realistic goals, and enjoy what they are doing.

Children need to be given every opportunity to feel successful. Small playing fields and goal nets help accomplish this in soccer. Basketball rims can be lowered. In individual sports such as skiing, all-terrain courses and team scoring can help more children feel a sense of accomplishment.

Lastly, parents should have fun with their children in sports. Practice together, but make it fun. Hit tennis balls, ski together, play catch. Vary routines and activities. Do other sporting activities as a family such as going on a bike trip, horseback riding, and hiking. Provide recreational alternatives to organized competition.

What makes the difference between youth sports participation being beneficial and harmful for children?

The answer to this question depends mainly on the attitudes and behaviors of the parents, coaches, and administrators of youth sports programs. Parents and coaches who take a positive approach to sports, who deemphasize winning, and who provide a healthy sport environment will make youth sports involvement a positive experience for children.

Rainer Martens, professor of sport psychology at the University of Illinois, has written an excellent book, *The Joy and Sadness of Children's Sports*, in which he summarizes the arguments for and against youth sports:

Yes, most certainly, children's sports should be celebrated, not indicted. Yet we cannot bury our heads in the sand: there are problems that require our attention. Just as athletes strive for excellence within sports, we should strive for sports programs to be excellent. . . . The overriding factor which supersedes all other concerns is the quality of adult leadership provided by the parents and coaches who guide these programs. (Martens 1978, p. 67)

The joy and the sadness of youth sports participation depend on the attitudes and behavior of the adults who run the programs and the type of influence parents have on their children. Parents who view athletics as an opportunity to be close to their children, to have fun as a family, and to use sports as a laboratory for setting and achieving goals will make sports a valuable experience. Parents who pressure their children beyond their ability or desire to achieve will make youth sports a negative experience.

Why do children drop out of competitive sports?

Daniel Gould and Thelma Horn (1984) have summarized the research that has been done in answer to this question. They state that children drop out of sports for a variety of reasons. Athletes over fourteen years old most frequently drop out because they develop other interests, such as cars, the opposite sex, music, drama, and friends. Also, this is the age where sports teams at school become highly selective. If they do not make the high school teams, children go in different directions, and often continue in sports activities on an informal basis.

Of particular interest, however, are the reasons why younger children drop out of sports. Children in the nine to fourteen age group do not drop out because of other interests. They quit sports mainly for two reasons: lack of playing time and the perception that they are not successful in their particular sports. These children are at the vulnerable age when they can evaluate themselves negatively if they do not feel they match up to their peers.

Parents must be careful, then, to choose athletic environments for their children where they will get adequate playing time and where they will not judge themselves as failures. There must be a good match between the child and the sports program. Playing on a team or in a league where the other children are at a higher skill level will not help the child's self-esteem.

Parents need to be sensitive to individual differences in their children's interests and temperaments. One child who is self-motivated and who thrives on competition will be more suited for highly competitive individual sports that require intensive training, such as gymnastics, skiing, and swimming. Another child in the same family may prefer a more low-keyed activity, such as the town youth soccer program.

One study of male child athletes (Griffin 1978) found that 90 percent of the boys would rather play on a losing team than sit on the bench of a winning team. This difference is important for parents to remember. Your child will likely prefer playing, and thus feeling successful, than being on a winning team, not playing, and feeling personally unsuccessful.

At what age should a child enter competition?

Fun-oriented competition can begin at any age. As a general rule, however, a child is not ready for intense competition and training until the onset of puberty and adolescence. Therefore, competition before age fourteen should be fun, with a minimum of win-lose pressure.

When a child has passed the pubertal growth spurt and has developed some emotional maturity, then more intense competition can begin. National rankings and intense competition for twelve- and thirteen-year-olds is unwise for two reasons. First, early success does not always correlate with future success. Many early maturers lose ground when they are older, and late maturers catch up. A child must be allowed to develop at the right pace and with the right balance. Second, intense pressure on this age group can easily lead to burnout. Parents and sports organizations should strive to help children enjoy the fun of the sport and not seek success based on national or regional rankings.

Though this general rule regarding intense competition for preadolescent children should be followed carefully by all parents, there are some exceptions to the rule. Some children under fourteen have a strong desire to compete. Unless they do so, they will become bored. They seek a greater challenge than do most of their peers. These children can enter a highly competitive environment earlier, but parents should be cautious and keep a watchful eye on the situation. Too much pressure at a vulnerable age can lead to burnout. Again, parents should seek a balance by matching the skills and personality of the child to the demands of that particular level of sports.

At what age should a child specialize in one sport?

A child should play a variety of sports, both team and individual, for as long as possible for three reasons. First, variety is an antidote for boredom: it can prevent burnout. Second, different sports require different skills, and a blending of various psychomotor skills results in a better all-around athlete. Early sport specialization creates a narrowly focused athlete. Third, participation in a variety of sports at an early age will help the child achieve a lifetime of sports participation.

How much time and money should parents spend on youth sports?

How much to spend is a hard question to answer, due largely to the variance in the financial and time requirements of some sports. Training, coaching, ice time, and traveling to meets can cost the parents of a young figure skater between $15,000 and $20,000 a year. Skiing can be equally as expensive if parents pay for a ski academy, some European summer camps, and travel to national events. At the opposite end of the continuum, youth soccer and basketball can cost $200 or less a year including equipment, entry fees, uniforms, and summer camp.

The decision on time and money needs to be based on a balance of four factors. First and probably most important, is the amount of money that the family has available to spend on recreation. Second, the financial requirements of the particular sport must be considered. Third, is the intensity of the child's desire to train and compete. And fourth, is the willingness of the parents to support the child in this area.

Outstanding athletes often have parents who provide extensive support for their athletic activities. Research on families of elite athletes indicates that parents are willing to spend large amounts of money for special coaching, equipment, and training opportunities. Benjamin Bloom and his colleagues (1985), for example, studied the home environments of young people who achieved the highest level of success in several fields, such as music, art, and athletics. As the children in these families developed their talents, parents would spend increasingly large sums of money on special training and traveling. Often a point would be reached where the family had to make considerable sacrifices to meet these expenses.

Parents of children who choose individual sports must realize that continued participation at high levels will require large amounts of time and money. Parents need to be careful not to encourage the child to continue unless they are willing to make large sacrifices. Parents for whom this is a problem might encourage the child in another sport for which the demands in family time and money are less.

A final word on money. Coaches and sport psychologists have witnessed many families in which parents control and manipulate their children with money. It is not uncommon to encounter young athletes who have been told by their parents that many sacrifices are being made by the entire family, and that the athletes had better pay this back somehow in the form of future earnings from sports or college scholarships. The guilt that results from such pressure is enormous, and is both damaging and limiting to the young athlete. If parents believe they are making some kind of investment in the future by supporting their son's or daughter's training, they are in dangerous waters. The best attitude to have is, "I am supporting you because I love you and I know you enjoy this activity. There are no strings attached."

Should I coach my own child?

Whether to coach one's own child must be dealt with separately in two areas of parental coaching: formal and informal.

Formal Coaching. Most recreational youth sports organizations, such as youth soccer, baseball, and basketball teams, are dependent on designated volunteer coaches, who are most often parents. It is also necessary for the success of these programs that parents be willing to coach. While there is no research to document this influence, casual observations indicate that in the majority of cases parental coaching is a positive experience for both parent and child. As long as parents maintain a proper balance of fun, skills development, and goal achievement, coaching is rewarding. There are many books that can help a parent learn how to be an effective coach. Perhaps the best—must reading for the inexperienced—is *Coaching Young Athletes* (Martens et al. 1981).

Parent coaches need to be acutely aware of one important principle: not to treat your child any differently from other children on the team. This principle applies to attendance at practice, actual play, and when disciplining for inappropriate behavior. A parent coach must avoid the extremes of favoritism, on the one hand, and excessive expectations, on the other.

There are some parents, however, who probably should not coach their own children. The extreme Persuader-type parent, who is results-oriented and does not see youth sports as a place for fun and skills development, should leave the coaching to someone else.

In individual sports such as skiing, skating, riding, and gymnastics it is generally not a good idea for parents to coach their youngsters. Few parents have the technical skills or the time for this kind of intense coaching, so parents should try to find a professionally certified and well-experienced coach. The parents' role is to support the coach, communicate frequently with him or her, and openly discuss problems or differences of opinion when they arise.

Informal Coaching. Informal coaching is parental advice, solicited or unsolicited, given to the young athlete with the goal of improving the athlete's technique, skill, or mental attitude. Informal coaching is usually offered before and after games, in the car, or at home.

All parents coach their children when they are young. Mothers and fathers enjoy teaching them to throw, hit, kick, and catch. This early involvement is the origin of informal parental coaching. For most young athletes there is a point, though, when they no longer appreciate their parents' telling them how to perform. This seems to be an individual matter. Some children do not like it all; others have mixed feelings about it. And the age at which it no longer is useful varies from child to child.

Don't Tell Us What to Do

I worked with a group of figure skaters who wanted to learn some sport psychology methods to cope with the pressures of training and competition. The topic often turned to the pressures they felt from their parents. I asked them to make a list of gripes. Number 3 on the list relates to coaching:

1. We don't like parents who live through their children.
2. We don't like parents who pay a professional to teach us and then yell at the pro or us.
3. Parents shouldn't try to tell us how [to do the skills required in our sport] when they have no idea what they're talking about.
4. When we're doing our best, a parent should not get on our nerves about trying harder.
5. When your kid competes, you shouldn't want him to win for you but for himself.

There is little research on how children react to their parents' giving advice. In one study (Hellstedt 1986), however, ski racers indicated that they reacted positively to informal parental coaching only when they perceived the parent to have skill and knowledge about the sport.

It appears, then, that parental coaching should be done with tact and only when the parent is knowledgeable or talented in that sport. Guidance and direction about skills that the parent has not experienced can be met with hostility or disinterest.

Are athletes born or made?

Both. Athletes are born *and* made, but learned personality traits are more important to athletic success than is genetic endowment. Certain physical skills and talents are required in every sport. Height and arm length are important for success in basketball. Speed and endurance are essential in track and field. Explosive muscle strength is important in football.

More important, however, is the psychological makeup of the athlete. Commitment to a goal and the willingness to work hard are the qualities that make an athlete successful. In this sense a good athlete is made.

The athlete develops these personality traits in a family environment where certain parental attitudes and values are present, namely, an emphasis on achievement, hard work, goal setting, and a positive approach to parenting.

The next chapter will help you develop a practical environment conducive to your child's successful youth sports experience.

REFERENCES

Bloom, Benjamin, ed. *Developing Talent in Young People.* New York: Ballantine, 1985.

Bunker, Linda and Robert Rotella. "Getting Them Up, Not Uptight." In *Youth Sports Guide for Coaches and Parents,* edited by Jerry Thomas. Reston, Va.: Amerian Alliance for Health, Physical Education, Recreation, and Dance, 1977.

Bushnell, Davis. "Burnout: Too Much, Too Soon." *Boston Globe,* 22 September 1986.

Gould, Daniel, and Thelma Horn. "Participation Motivation in Young Athletes." In *Psychological Foundations of Sport,* edited by J. Silva and R. Weinberg. Champaign, Ill.: Human Kinetics, 1984.

Greene, Robert. "Only 9 and He Knows It." *Boston Globe,* 6 August 1981.

Griffin, L. "Why Children Participate in Youth Sports." Paper presented at American Alliance for Health, Physical Education, Recreation, and Dance conference, Kansas City, Missouri, 1978.

Hellstedt, Jon. "Family Charactertstics of Ski Racers," Unpublished paper, 1986.

Martens, Rainer. *The Joy and Sadness in Children's Sports.* Champaign, Ill.: Human Kinetics, 1978.

Martens, Rainer, Robert Christina, John Harvey, and Brian Sharkey. *Coaching Young Athletes.* Champaign, Ill.: Human Kinetics, 1981.

Passer, Michael. "Competitive Trait Anxiety in Children and Adolescents." In *Psychological Foundations of Sport,* edited by J. Silva and R. Weinberg. Champaign, Ill.: Human Kinetics, 1984.

Rotella, Robert, and Linda Bunker. *Parenting Your Superstar.* Champaign, Ill.: Leisure Press, 1987.

Scanlan, Tara. "Competitive Stress and the Child Athlete." In *Psychological Foundations of Sport,* edited by J. Silva and R. Weinberg. Champaign, Ill.: Human Kinetics, 1984.

Smith, M. "Hockey Violence: Interning Some Myths." In *Sport Psychology: An Analysis of Athlete Behavior,* edited by W. Straub. Ithaca, N.Y.: Mouvement, 1980.

Smith, Ronald, and Frank Smoll. "Psychological Stress: A Conceptual Model and Some Intervention Strategies in Youth Sports." In *Chil-*

dren in Sport: A Contemporary Anthology, edited by R. Magill, M. Ash, and F. Smoll. Champaign, Ill.: Human Kinetics, 1982.

Smolev, Barry. "The Relationship between Sport and Aggression." In The Humanistic and Mental Health Aspects of Sport, Exercise, and Recreation, edited by T. Craig. Chicago: American Medical Association, 1976.

Chapter 4

Steps to the Enabler's Circle

by Jon C. Hellstedt, Ph.D.

An Enabler is a parent who provides a child with the support, opportunity, and power to make things happen. In sports an enabling parent provides what the child needs to accomplish his or her goals, whether these goals involve becoming an Olympic champion or a happy, recreational tennis player.

The Enabler's circle is a moment in time, and it is the product of your role as an enabling parent. It is the time in your relationship with your athletic child when you both feel you have reached your goals. It is when you feel proud of your child, and when your child appreciates the support and encouragement you have given through the years.

Within the circle is intimacy, warmth, and mutual respect. You and your child experience a reciprocal feeling of joy at a job well done, regardless of win, loss, or rank.

The Second Run

A personal moment in the Enabler's circle occurred when my sixteen-year-old daughter was competing in the Eastern Freestyle Ski Championships.

It's the day of the event, and my daughter needs a good ballet run to make it to the National Championships. She's had an up-and-down season, so she needs a good score to qualify. She's noticeably tense before the first run. The result is a disaster. She falls twice, assuring her of a low score.

At the bottom of the run she's crying so hard she can hardly breathe. I dash to her, and watch as a few friends try to comfort her. She continues to cry. My guts feel heavy, like I've just swallowed a brick. I want to cry, but I won't let myself. I try to comfort her as she is still on the snow. I touch her shoulder and offer to help her up, but I don't say anything. What is there to say? Nothing seems to fit right now. My camera hangs like a dead and useless object around my neck.

She gets up after regaining her ability to breath normally. I utter some empty words, like, "It's all right, honey." She avoids listening, and skis off to prepare herself for the second run. She seems to want to be alone.

I dread watching the second run. It's all or nothing. I think of all kinds of rationalizations to accept the defeat when it comes, the main one being, This isn't all that important, anyhow. But to her it is. Making the nationals is the most important thing in her life right now. More important than boys, college—everything.

This is it, I say to myself as she begins her run. I clutch my camera. I try to look calm. All the way down the course I fear that she's going to fall, but she doesn't. She skis beautifully on her second run. My fear turns to joy.

I walk back to the lodge feeling as if I'm bouncing on the snow. I'm so excited for her. She has worked so hard. She's not a first-place finisher, but she has met her goal. She's done what she has set out to do.

Later she sits on my lap in the lodge, and we share the joy of the moment. I share with her my pride and excitement. I can tell she feels good about what I had just said.

The years of driving her to meets, paying the bills, comforting her at times of previous defeats, frustrations, and heartaches pass quickly through my mind. It's all worth the price right now.

Parents can achieve the Enabler's circle by unreservedly accepting both their child's triumphs and defeats, home runs and strikeouts. In the Enabler's circle there are no losers.

Pat Van Buskirk wrote about such a moment in a story originally published in *Woman's Day* and later reprinted in *Joy and Sadness in Children's Sports* (Martens 1978). She describes how her son, lacking the physical skills of other children on the Little League team, worked hard all season long, played infrequently, made errors, and repeatedly struck out. In the last game of the season, however, his hard work is rewarded when he catches a crucial fly ball. She concludes her story with this description of the Enabler's circle:

Baseball season is ending now and, at this moment, Johnny is asleep. He lies on his back, arms outstretched and limp. There is a football carefully placed beside his pillow. (Oh Lord, give me strength.) I lean over to kiss the soft curve of his little-boy cheek and an idea occurs to me. I think of other mothers who sit in stands and cheer sons who hit homers and win medals. It must be great to be the mother of a winner, but I decided it couldn't be half as heartwarming and tender an experience as mothering a gallant little loser. (P. 332)

These two parental experiences reflect the joys of being a parent of an athlete. Dealing with a child in such situations requires skill, patience, and sound judgment. The wrong words or behavior could have negative consequences. To minimize the negative outcomes for your children and family, you should follow seven basic steps toward reaching the Enabler's circle.

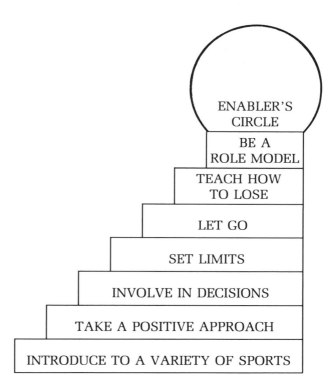

Figure 4.1   Steps to the Enabler's circle.

Step 1: Introduce Your Child to a Variety of Sports

Expose your child early to a variety of sports. Team sports give children a chance to learn how to play in company and interact with their peers. Under proper adult supervision, team sports programs are usually lots of fun for young children.

Individual sports provide a healthy complement to team sports. They offer a different environment, one in which the child can set his or her own goals and develop individual skills.

Prior to six years of age a child can be taught to play in an informal sports environment. Catching and throwing, hitting a large ball, jumping rope, and playing other hand-eye coordination games such as Frisbee are good ways to introduce a child to sports. Individual sports such as skiing and gymnastics can start at this time, too. Team sports such as soccer and youth baseball or softball can begin at age six or seven, depending on local resources.

There is a certain self-selection process that goes on with children. Because of their unique body build and temperament, children are predisposed to one or more types of sports. For example, one child in a family may have the characteristics for participation in football. Another may prefer a more solitary activity such as running or long-distance swimming. By exposing your children early to a variety of team and individual sports, you establish a basis on which they can select the activities that will interest them as they grow older.

It is not a good idea, however, to have all your child's free time spent in organized youth sports programs. Participation in too many organized programs at once can actually damage the child's sense of playtime with overstructure. The young athlete will learn to depend on fun as being only structured and lose the creative ability at self-play.

Seek a balance between organized and spontaneous play. Backyard games are valuable because the child learns how to create games by his or her own rules, without the fancy equipment, uniforms, and clearly defined rules of organized sports. Organized youth sports, on the other hand, give children more formal structure and coaching that will enhance skills development. Children need both types of play environments.

Step 2: Motivate Your Child With a Positive Approach

Motivation is the degree of effort an individual puts forth to achieve a goal. In athletics—as in academics, music, and art—motivation is of prime importance. Successful athletes are motivated athletes.

As parents we all want our children to be successful. Consequently, many parents struggle with the issue of how they can help their child develop motivation.

Parents need to realize that they can not *create* motivation in their children. However, there are some things you can do that will create a motivation-enhancing environment within your family. The key is to create an atmosphere in which your children feel good about themselves, set their own goals, and get rewarded for accomplishing them.

Following are some suggestions for creating this kind of healthy environment.

Take a positive approach. Your most effective tool for motivating your children is praise. Positive acknowledgment of their accomplishments creates a warm feeling that will continue to motivate them.

Praising

The examples below demonstrate three ingredients in a positive verbal reward statement. The "I" message is followed by an expression of feeling (pride, excitement, joy), which is then followed by a behavioral description of what skills you see being improved. It is important to specify the behavior for two reasons. First, it gives the child concrete feedback; and second, it gives the child the knowledge that you are not offering empty praise. You really mean what you are saying.

I am proud of you. You played well today.

I'm excited about your progress in tennis. Your shots are really improving.

I enjoy playing ball with you. You're learning to catch the ball really well.

I love you.

The frequency of your verbal rewards should vary with the developmental stage of your child. In early stages (through middle childhood) reward frequently and generously. As he or she gets older (later childhood and adolescence), reward less frequently and only when performance merits it.

Even with older children and adolescents, praise is best given in response to specific behavior. A high school basketball player will benefit more from a specific behavioral praise such as "Your rebounding was excellent tonight," as opposed to a general comment such as "Good game."

In giving praise, avoid dishonesty. A statement such as "You played well today" after a game in which your daughter struck out three times and made the game-losing error will not help your credibility as a parent. But a statement such as "If you feel disappointed about the game, I understand how you feel" gives your child the message that you are honest and that your approval means something.

Use nonverbal rewards. Verbal rewards are good. But nonverbal recognition can make your child-athlete feel even better. A hug or a pat on the shoulder can communicate more than mere words.

Touch your children frequently. You can't do it enough. The approval communicated by that touch will remain for a long time.

Minimize material rewards. Unfortunately, some parents believe that offering material rewards such as money or gifts will improve performance. Research has shown that such rewards do not motivate and, in fact, may dampen a desire for self-improvement because the desired reward becomes external and not internal. In addition, such a reward system may result in your child's being the object of jokes from the other children. "A dollar for every hit" will have no effect on your child's batting average.

A more valuable reward is the spontaneous offer of a treat. "You guys played so well today, I feel like taking you out for an ice cream cone" is the kind of material reward that children appreciate. Use it only on special occasions, however, or it loses its value.

Avoid negative rewards: criticism and punishment. Parents often think they can motivate their child by using criticism or by withholding love or affection. Psychological research has found that these methods do not work. In fact, they create a high level of anxiety in a child that can have negative consequences in athletic performance.

Parents who accuse their child of not working hard enough when they are training four or more times a week for their figure-skating or gymnastics events, for example, are discouraging that child. If you see that your child is not putting in the effort he or she is capable of, sit down together and say, "You don't seem to have your heart in what you're doing. Is there something bugging you right now?" This will get better results than telling your child that he or she is not hustling.

Some coaches and parents also use punishment. Taking a player out of the game when he or she has just made a mistake is a form of punishment, as is criticism for not hustling during the game. For younger children (under fourteen) there is limited value to punishments in sport; they should rarely be used by either parents or coaches.

The best negative reward is your threat to deprive them of something they want to do in the future. Take, for example, poor conduct on the tennis court. It is useful for a parent to say, "If you throw your racket again in a match, I'm not going to let you play in the next tournament." Threatened punishments must be implemented if the violation occurs, however, or they are of little value.

Determine what you mean by *success.* In sports "success" is a word that is used to describe a desired outcome or goal. A *successful* athlete is one who performs at a certain established level. Success is often a very subjective feeling. Many athletes are good at what they do, yet they do not feel successful. Others accomplish less and feel successful. What accounts for this difference? Often it is the realistic or unrealistic expectations by which the athlete measures performance. An important source of these personal expectations is standards set by the parents in the home environment. Parents can help their children feel good about themselves by setting reasonable and achievable standards for measuring success.

There are two measures of success. The first is success measured by objective standards. The standard most often used in sports is winning and losing. Winning is a successful performance; losing is an unsuccessful one. When this standard is used to measure performance, success is based on outcome.

Unfortunately, many parents use this standard. The child who makes the team or wins the tennis tournament is successful; the child who does not is not successful. The young athletes who make the top hockey team are *good;* those who do not are *not good.* Since so few make it to the top in athletics, outcome is not a valuable criterion for determining success.

Sometimes in families this standard is used when an older sister's or brother's performance is used as a benchmark. An older sister may have made the varsity soccer team as a freshman. If her parents expect the same of other children, the younger sister will feel unsuccessful if she does not follow suit. She will feel a sense of failure, even though she is a capable athlete. Or if she makes the team, she may not feel it is an unusual accomplishment. She may feel it is expected of her.

Therefore, it is better for parent and athlete alike to define success on the basis of self-improvement. This approach individualizes performance. The child is evaluated on his or her own performance, not that of some other person or group. The young athlete uses prior performance as a baseline and any improvement from that level of performance is successful. For example, at the beginning of the swimming season a child swims the fifty-yard freestyle in thirty-five seconds and two weeks later swims the same distance in thirty-four. Because the child's performance has improved, he or she has been successful. The standard for success is the child's own performance in skills acquisition and development.

If you adopt self-improvement as a standard for success in your family, each of your children will be able to be evaluated by his or her own performance standards, and the child's chances for developing positive self-worth will increase.

Rewarding Self-improvement

Your child will develop competence as you reward new skills. The same child, however, will develop a negative self-concept if new skills are not rewarded or the child is negatively compared to others.

An eleven-year-old girl in a recreational basketball program, for example, will feel a sense of competence when:

- Her father tells her she has improved her free-throw shooting since the beginning of the season.
- Her mother tells her she is learning how to be a team player by passing the ball more often than she did in the last game.
- Her parents comment on how she is holding her hands up more on defense.

The girl will develop a sense of incompetence and frustration when:

- Her father tells her she is not playing as well as another girl on the team.
- Her parents tell her she is not hustling.
- Her father gets angry and yells from the bleachers when she misses a key basket.

Set self-improvement goals. A good youth sports coach can help the child develop skills. Learning how to shoot, pass, dribble, and play good defense should be far more important than winning the league championship.

Research has found that coaches who are most liked by their team members are those who are good teachers. John Wooden, the coach of UCLA during the years of consistent national championships, was a master teacher of skills. If he criticized a player, he would immediately follow the scold with an instruction about how to execute the move properly. He never told his team that they should go out and win.

You cannot find a player who ever played for me at UCLA that can tell you that he ever heard me mention "winning" a basketball game. He might say I inferred a little here and there, but I never mentioned winning. Yet the last thing that I told my players, just prior to tipoff, before we would go on the floor, was, "When the game is over, I want your head up—and I know of only one way for your head to be up—and that's for you to know that you did your best. . . . This means to do the best YOU can do. That's the best; no one can do more. . . . You made that effort." (Tharp and Gallimore 1976, p. 78)

Parents can learn from John Wooden, too. Reward effort rather than outcome. Help your children feel good about their improvement.

The best way to work on their improvement goals is to get involved yourself, physically. Go outside with your children and help them practice. Gently encourage them to work on weaknesses that need improvement. If your son is a goalie in soccer, offer to kick shots to him so he can practice his saves. Hit tennis balls to your daughter's backhand if that is her weakness. Do not coach her, however, unless you know the technical aspects of the game, but compliment her when she makes a good shot.

Set realistic goals. If the goal is to be reached it must be realistic. Having unrealistic goals leads to frustration and a sense of failure. It is helpful for a parent to discuss with a child what his or her goals are for the season and together determine whether these goals are achievable. An ideal goal is one that is beyond the present level of skill but not unreachable.

A parent should have a practical sense of the child's ability. Then the parent can help the child set realistic goals. If the child is just learning a new sport, it is unlikely that he or she will make the top team in that age group. Sound parental advice can help this child set a realistic goal of making one of the lower-level teams.

The Unrealistic Parent

A father of a fifteen-year-old boy called the coach at a ski academy and asked if his child could apply for admission. The coach said yes, and then asked for some more information on the boy's skiing background and ability. The father said that the boy had just begun skiing but had already done well in some local races. He went on to say that he would like the boy to get some intensive ski training and hoped that this would help him make the U.S. ski team.

Sound silly? Perhaps so. But many parents set unrealistic goals for their children, especially when a child first enters a sport. Parents should educate themselves about the sport before committing the child to what could turn out to be a frustrating and disappointing experience for all.

Keep it fun. If sports are fun, children will want to continue. If they no longer are fun, who would want to play? Keeping perspective on the role of fun will help motivate the child.

Practice sessions with your children need to be fun. If your daughter gets angry at herself or at you, there is a problem. Examine it. Are you pushing too hard? If so, let go. Play a game while hitting tennis balls to each other: ten in a row and she gets a point; three points and you buy the ice cream.

Emphasize hard work. Success at anything in life involves hard work. Terry Orlick, in his book *In Pursuit of Excellence* (1980), reports the results of a survey of NHL coaches that asked what personal ingredient is most important in making it to the professional level of hockey. The responses were most often words such as *desire, heart,* and *determination.* The coaches agreed that what makes an athlete great is a desire to work hard.

Bloom's study (1985) of the home influences on successful athletes found that in almost all families the parents emphasized hard work and achievement. The most often-heard phrase in growing up was "A job worth doing is worth doing well."

Emphasize working to meet the goals your children set for themselves. Parents need to remind children to continue to strive for improvement, because children will sometimes seek a comfortable level of performance and not challenge themselves.

It is important to find a balance here, too. You will not profit from constantly preaching or beating them over the head with the work-ethic message. Gentle and timely reminders work better.

Separate being and doing. Even though the emphasis is on rewarding self-improvement, parents need to remember that how a child does in a sports event should not be confused with the child's self-worth. If a child strikes out in the last of the ninth with the bases loaded, he or she is still a good person. A child should never feel that self-worth is dependent on performance. Self-worth is based on their value as a person (being), not on how they perform (doing).

Confront undesirable behavior. It is helpful for children for you to confront them when they are not meeting their own goals. Confrontation, however, is not necessary until your child approaches adolescence. When the child reaches this stage, you will have to confront him or her on occasion. For example, if your fourteen-year-old son is a ski racer who is on an off-season training schedule set up by the coaches, you may need to help him keep to the schedule. Do not force him to train. Confront him when he is not doing it by reminding him of his commitments to himself and his coach. Giving him an external structure is a temporary aid until he develops his own internal control mechanisms.

The danger, of course, is pushing too hard. *Gentle* confrontation is suggested. Stick to the facts. It is their program. Ask, "What can I do to help you work out this week?" Push gently but firmly. A study of ski racers (Hellstedt 1986) indicated that the racers generally responded favorably to their parents' influencing them to stick to their training schedules. Many indicated that this intervention helped them reach their goals.

There are times when your child will need firm direction from you.

When these situations arise—verbal aggression during a game, crying inappropriately, blaming others such as referees or coaches for their own mistakes—a firm confrontation is warranted.

Confrontation Guidelines

1. Confront behavior around the sport, not mistakes in the game itself.

2. Wait until after the game to confront your child privately, not in front of other children.

3. Follow the format of describing the undesirable behavior, your own feelings about that behavior, and what changes you would like to see. Take, for example, the case of the twelve-year-old soccer player who gets taken out of the game by the coach, and then instead of standing with the other team members around the coach, goes off by himself and pouts. On the way home his father says, "I didn't like it when you went off by yourself and acted disgusted at being taken out of the game. Your coach and teammates probably don't like it either. Next time you get taken out and are upset, I want you to stand with the other players and continue to watch the game."

4. Follow a confrontation (such as the case above) with a statement about how you love your child and care for him or her but are upset with his or her behavior in that specific area.

Attend games and events. One of the most important rewards your children will receive from you is your recognition that their activities are important. Your attendance at their games and events indicates your support and concern for them.

Most young athletes enjoy having their parents watch them perform. A study conducted on fifteen- and sixteen-year-old ski racers (Hellstedt 1986), for example, showed that over 60 percent of the respondents liked their parents to watch them race "very much." Only 12 percent indicated a preference for their parents not to watch them compete. The racers also preferred their parents to watch them "right on the race course" (75 percent) as opposed to watching from the base lodge (14 percent). Although these figures are from one sport only, they indicate a child's satisfaction in having parents there, and in close proximity to the actual event.

Go to as many games, races, and competitions as you can. Do not feel guilty if you miss something, however. You can not possibly attend all events, and your child should have the experience of performing without your being present. Explain your reasons if you can not be there. If a big event is coming up, ask your child if he or she wants you to be there.

If the answer is yes, try to change your plans.

A general rule to follow is, the younger the child, the more important it is that you attend games. As the child matures, you can miss more games, but try not to miss more than half of the games, even when your son or daughter enters adolescence.

There are some athletes who do not like their parents to attend events, perhaps because it puts too much pressure on them or, in rare cases, because of a history of negative experiences with their parents.

Reservations

Some young athletes have reservations about their parents attending events.

A nationally ranked diver said to me, "Yes, I like it when my parents come. But not when they say things about how much it cost to come to the meet. Then if I do poorly, I feel guilty."

Another competitor said, "I get uptight when my parents come and watch me compete. It's not that I don't love them. I do. It's that I want to please them so much, I get really nervous when they are there."

So, it is always a good idea to discuss your attendance at crucial events with your son or daughter. In some cases your presence may be stressful to the child. Find out how your child feels about it.

Your behavior at athletic events is also important to your child. Your son or daughter may not always tell you, but he or she is concerned about how you appear and act. This consciousness is especially true with the adolescent competitor for whom peer approval is important and for whom your behavior can be a considerable source of embarrassment.

Behavior at Team Sports Events

1. Your child may not like it when you yell. So try not to yell at all.

2. Don't ever yell critical comments at your child. If you must yell, do so with encouraging statements. "Nice shot," "Way to go," and "Good job" are examples. Otherwise be quiet. Few, if any, children like it when they can hear their own parents' voices above all others.

3. Never yell at members of the other team, the other coaches, or the referees. Let other parents make fools of themselves.

4. Don't try to talk to your child at halftime to give quick instructions on strategy or tactics. Let the coach do that. Your suggestions place additional pressure on your child and make him or her more nervous.

5. Act dignified in victory and defeat. Congratulate the losing team and praise the winning team members.

6. Have fun driving to games and events. Show your child that you enjoy this process. Avoid the pep talks and lectures about putting out 110 percent. Stop for ice cream on the way home. Tell jokes. Laughter is great therapy.

Behavior at Individual Sports Events

1. Act calm yourself. Your child needs to be relaxed to perform well. Your tension will be infectious.

2. Don't instruct your child. Encourage him or her to do well. Please, no tips on how to improve performance. It's too late for that.

3. Bring a newspaper or magazine to help you relax during pauses in the action.

4. If you have time to talk in between events, keep it relaxed and light. Have fun together.

5. If your son or daughter does poorly during the first event, encourage your child to do better in the second. Don't point out your child's mistakes or give a strategy for the second event. This will only confuse your child.

6. At the end of the competition, regardless of the outcome, reward your child's effort with verbal and nonverbal rewards. Remember, an affectionate hug will do more than a lot of words.

7. Have fun yourself. Get to know the other parents. Joke with them. Don't take everything so seriously. Talk about things other than your child's standing in the sport.

Step 3: Involve Your Child in Decision-Making

The Bill of Rights for Young Athletes, published by the American Alliance for Health, Physical Education, Recreation, and Dance, enumerates ten principles of ethical propriety in youth sports programs. One of these, the fifth, is the right of each child to share in the leadership and decision-making of his or her sport participation.

Bill of Rights for Young Athletes

1. Right to participate in sports regardless of ability level.
2. Right to participate at a level that is commensurate with each child's developmental level.
3. Right to have qualified adult leadership.
4. Right to participate in safe and healthy environments.

5. Right of each child to share in the leadership and decision-making of their sport participation.
6. Right to play as a child and not as an adult.
7. Right to proper preparation for participation in the sport.
8. Right to an equal opportunity to strive for success.
9. Right to be treated with dignity by all involved.
10. Right to have fun through sport.

What does this right mean for the decision-making process in athletic families? How can it be applied to the many decisions that must be made regarding sports participation?

There are three basic styles of decision-making in families. Parents who are Persuaders often use an authoritarian method. In this style the decisions are made by the parents and imposed on the child. The power is from the top down. The problem with this style of decision-making is that it does not value the opinions and wishes of the child.

Persuader Decision-Making

• A father believes that football is the best sport for his son, and he strongly influences the boy to play football even though the boy enjoys soccer.
• Skiing parents might say to their children, "We don't want you to do other winter sports, we ski as a family."
• Parents who believe that basketball is too "masculine" insist that their daughter participate in gymnastics.

There are times and situations, especially when children are young, when decisions need to be made by parental authority. When parents honestly believe that their decision is correct, the authoritarian style is appropriate. An example would be a decision to withdraw a child from sports because the playing conditions are not safe and there is danger of serious physical or emotional injury.

Parents who are Avoiders use a laissez-faire approach. This style leaves the children to make their own decisions with little or no parental input.

Avoider Decision-Making

• A child wants to quit her soccer team after a few weeks because she feels the coach doesn't play her enough. Mom and Dad tell her, "It's your decision, do whatever you want."
• A fourteen-year-old boy who weighs 120 pounds and is a very good soccer player decides to go out for the high school football team instead of the soccer team. His parents let him make that decision

with little discussion of the danger of injury.

• A sixteen-year-old basketball player is put on a strength-building program by her coach during the summer. The young athlete starts out following the program for two weeks, then gradually stops her workouts. Her parents don't say anything about this, and let her noncompliance go without confrontation.

Though parental involvement in decision-making must decrease as the child grows older, even at full maturity parental input should be heard and listened to. Children should not make decisions without discussion with parents. An avoidance of discussing these issues shows a lack of interest on the part of the parents.

The style of decision-making that Enablers use is consensus. Consensus reflects shared influence, respect, and power. Consensual decision-making is characterized by the parents' seeking the opinions of everyone concerned with the problem and arriving at a mutually satisfying decision.

The steps in consensual decision-making are (1) define the problem; (2) gather information; (3) analyze the information; (4) propose a solution; (5) negotiate if far apart; (6) agree to a solution; and (7) evaluate the decision at a later time.

Following are two typical situations that parents of athletic children might encounter. Each method of decision-making will be applied to the case study.

Dan, the Disgruntled Hockey Player

Dan, a twelve-year-old, informs his parents that he wants to quit his hockey team shortly after the season has begun.

If Dan's parents were Persuaders, they would say no, then add, "Hockey is good for you. Your older brothers played and they got a lot out of it. We want you to play also."

If they were Avoiders, they would say, "OK. If you want to quit, go ahead." Little discussion or debate would take place, either because his parents highly value Dan's making his own decisions or because his parents have little interest in sports.

In this case, however, Dan's parents used the Enabler's consensus model of decision-making, and followed these steps:

1. Define the problem: They listen to their son and discover that he likes the game of hockey, but does not get to play all that much and does not want to sit on the bench.

2. Gather information: Dan's parents explain their belief that playing on the first line is not as important as learning skills. They explain that Dan is one of the younger children on the team, and that

as he develops his skating ability and strength, he will get to play more. They explain that he made a commitment to playing this year and he should follow through on that commitment.

Dan responds that he thinks he is not as good as the other kids on the team and that the coach does not value his potential contribution.

Dan's parents talk to the coach, and he expresses his belief that the boy needs to work on some basic skills, and that when his skating and stick handling improve, he will get more ice time. He further explains that all the boys get to play a certain number of minutes, and that rule will apply to Dan as it applies to everyone else.

3. Analyze the information: The pros and cons of each position are considered. Dan expresses his feelings further about not wanting to continue even though he made the commitment. His parents point out the problems it would cause the team if he were to quit. They also explain the coach's opinion to Dan.

4. Propose a solution: Dan's parents propose that he continue and that at the end of the season they reevaluate the situation. If the boy does not want to continue the following season, they will respect his decision.

5. Negotiation is not necessary in this case.

6. Agree to a solution: Dan agrees to continue, with the understanding that his parents will respect the decision he makes at the end of the season.

7. Evaluate the decision: As the season progresses, Dan's parents periodically discuss with him how he is doing and whether he feels his skills are improving. At the end of the season Dan decides not to continue with hockey, and his parents support the decision.

Suzy, the Soccer (or Softball) Player

Suzy, a thirteen-year-old, has played both spring soccer and softball the past four seasons. Her parents feel that she is too busy with the two sports and that she needs to limit herself to just one. Her parents propose this to her two weeks before the signups.

Persuaders would decide what they want Suzy to do and communicate their verdict to her. If their decision is that she play only softball, they will give her no other options. Perhaps they would let her choose between the two sports, but her choices have to conform with their guidelines.

Avoiders would let Suzy choose whatever she wants. She might have to provide her own transportation, however, because they may not have the time or interest to car pool to practices and games. She must decide, but without their support.

Suzy's parents, however, followed these steps:

1. Define the problem: Suzy wants to play both sports. Her parents believe that she is overextended and would like her to limit herself to one sport.

2. Gather information: Her parents explain their position. Suzy's participation in two sports is a problem for them and the rest of the family. Often practices overlap; sometimes weekend games are scheduled at the same time. Her younger sister and brother have games and practices that require driving and car pooling. It is simply too much of a strain.

Suzy explains that she loves both sports, has friends that will be doing both, and has talked to the director of both programs. The directors have assured her that she can do both and that necessary adjustments can be made with her coaches.

3. Analyze the information: A discussion of the issues takes place. Suzy's parents explain that they are concerned about her schoolwork. Her grades have not been as high as they had been, and they feel she is under too much time pressure already. Playing one spring sport would ease some of that pressure.

Suzy explains that she does not think time is the problem. She has the time for both sports and her studies, but admits she has been lax in some of her subjects during the past marking period.

4. Propose a solution: Suzy proposes that she be allowed to do both. Her parents think it over, and come back two days later with a no, but indicate they are willing to talk further.

5. Negotiate if far apart: Suzy's parents suggest a compromise. They propose that she participate in both sports, but under the following conditions: (1) she agrees to ride her bike to practices and some games; (2) she explains to both coaches that she is doing two sports, but if her grades slip, some modification may have to be made; and (3) she maintains at least a B average on her progress reports from school or she will have to give up one sport.

6. Suzy agrees to the solution.

7. Evaluate the decision: Every two weeks Suzy and her parents talk about how the solution is working. Teacher conferences are held every four weeks to evaluate her academic progress.

Unlike the Persuader and Avoider approaches, the Enabler approach allows children to express their opinions. Both sides of an issue are discussed and differences are clarified. Children feel that they have a say in the decisions that are made. Both parents and children feel like winners.

But what happens when there is a stalemate? If there is no room for further negotiation, it is the responsibility of the parents to make the final decision. At times like these, parents can be *authoritative* without being *authoritarian*.

Being authoritative is using your authority as a parent in a rational manner after you have weighed the alternatives. An authoritarian parent does not listen to the issues but makes decisions from a set of values that are not changeable.

In the first example, if Dan was not willing to finish the hockey season, his parents would have to decide on the basis of their own personal value system which was more important: Dan's finishing his commitment or his giving up the sport and pursuing other interests. If one of the family rules, which had been articulated and followed in other situations, was that you finish what you start, Dan's parents would have required him to finish the season.

In the second example, if Suzy was not willing to reach a compromise, her parents might have decided that she had to limit herself to one sport. Though Suzy might not like the decision, she would probably feel that she had been listened to and that her parents' decision was a rational one.

Rules of Decision-Making

1. Children have a right to share in the decision-making regarding their sport participation.

2. If you have a tendency to be a Persuader, pay special attention to your children's side of the issue.

3. If you have a tendency to be an Avoider, don't be afraid to make decisions that are not popular with your children. You may have to decide for them until they reach maturity. You need to guide them and influence them at times.

4. Any decision involving one child in the family affects everyone else in some way. Consider the effect on the entire family as part of the data-gathering process.

5. The more time you spend talking with your children, listening to their side of the issue, and explaining how you feel, the easier it will be to arrive at a mutually acceptable decision.

6. When all attempts to negotiate a mutually acceptable decision come to a stalemate, you are the boss, and must make the decision.

Step 4: Set Limits and Enforce Rules

An athletic life is a disciplined life. A child can not become a good athlete without learning self-control, discipline, and the ability to manage time. Parents should teach these principles at an early age and maintain continuity between lessons.

Lessons begin, for example, when your seven-year-old daughter has a soccer game on Saturday morning and asks you if she can have a friend sleep over on Friday night. Your answer of no plants a seed. It tells her that sleep and relaxing the night before a game are important. Telling her instead that she can have her friend over on Saturday night gives her the message that an athletic life is not without fun. Gratification must be delayed at important times.

When your eight-year-old son wants to skip baseball practice to go to an amusement park, your no also gives him an important message: practice is important. You can not play in games if you are not willing to practice. His commitment to the team also requires his attendance at the practices.

Your fifteen-year-old daughter has a big test two days from now. She has field hockey practice after school, and needs to study in the evenings. She asks you if she can go to a party the evening before her test. Your no tells her that studies come first. She must structure her time to acomplish her important tasks.

These limits need to be based on a consistent set of family rules. A well-functioning family needs to have a set of rules that govern family members' behavior.

One Family's Rules

Each family must define its own set of rules. Rules are principles that govern behavior, and are taught openly and clearly to all members of the family.

Here are some examples of one family's rules that have application to athletics:

1. All children in our family have talents and activities they enjoy. As parents we will support your choice of activity that you wish to pursue intensively.

2. Accomplishing goals involves hard work.

3. Finish what you start. You don't quit halfway through the season. Remember, too, that for every rule there are exceptions. Two acceptable ones are poor academic performance and exposure to conditions that are not safe, including emotionally or physically abusive coaches.

4. Observe proper bedtimes and nutrition.

5. Studies come first.

6. Respect the rights of others. This rule applies to other players, referees, coaches, and family members.

Construct your own list. Put it on the refrigerator door.

Step 5: Let Go

There are times when your children need to be free of your influence. They benefit by handling new situations by themselves. Exposure to coaches and other adults in sports gives them other role models from which they can learn.

Do not expect the coach to agree with everything you believe. Your son's tennis coach may not have the same values about life that you hold. He may attempt to motivate your son in a different way than you do. He may want your son to change his stroke. This seeming contradiction between philosophies may result in a temporary drop in your son's performance. But it is not the end of the world. Your son may benefit from the new learning and from the experience of frustration at not winning.

At the stage of late childhood and certainly by early adolescence you need to begin letting go. Do it gradually. Let your child travel with others. Let your child be exposed to challenging competitions without your presence to support them. Your child needs to learn to trust his or her own inner resources. You can not always be there.

One way to let go is to allow the coach to be the coach and you the parent. After your child passes puberty you are not the technical expert. The coach is the one that provides that knowledge. Your role is to continue to foster character development on and off the field. Your role is helping to shape the child's behavior, not his or her athletic performance.

Step 6: Teach Your Child How to Lose

Hugh Armstrong (1986) said that it is more important to teach athletic children how to lose than it is to teach them how to win. What Armstrong really means is to teach them how to *accept* loss.

Losing is inevitable in sports. There is always someone better. Sometimes luck plays a part. A gust of wind or some ruts and ice on a ski racing course can mean the difference between winning and losing.

A young athlete must believe that losing is not failure. Losing is a part of life. It is a valuable lesson to learn from participation in sports.

When children learn how to lose they learn to cope with the pain and loneliness of defeat, and to know that there are better times ahead. Parents can help children deal with loss by not blaming poor performance on referees, coaches, or other players. Children need to see that loss is often due to lack of effort or training, and can be corrected by improvement in mental or physical skill. Teach them that is it OK to lose if the effort is there.

The following story by Jim Loehr (1986) describes a sensitive set of parents of an athlete who collapsed under pressure.

The Pressure Cooker

Such was the case with one of our nation's most promising young juniors. Marco Cacopardo has always been an excellent competitor. A top nationally ranked sixteen-and-under player, Marco has managed the pressure of competition well, according to his parents. But, as inevitably happens, Marco was treated to an extra-special dose of what we call pressure.

It all began at the Junior Davis Cup tryouts last July. Marco was playing well, winning matches, cruising. And then, out of the blue, it happened. Playing a pivotal match against Martin Blackman to make the team, Marco led 5-2 in the third set, serving at 40-15. Suddenly, he became so nervous he could hardly move. His muscles tightened, his heart raced out of control, the chemistry of fear dominated his physiology.

After the match Marco felt lower than ever. "I felt like totally quitting the game. I honestly believed I couldn't play the game any more. My future was over."

Marco's parents also witnessed his agony. "We had never seen anything like that before," said his mother, Sheila. "We felt hopeless and very concerned."

Parents play a critical role in properly managing this type of situation; Marco's parents did exactly the right thing. They took the pressure off completely: They listened, understood, accepted and never judged. Although they didn't understand what was happening, they just went with the feelings Marco had.

"Marco's feelings were first and foremost, and tennis was clearly secondary," said his mother. "We told him that whatever he wanted to do was OK. If he never played again, it would be OK with us; we just wanted him to be healthy and happy."

Marco's confidence began to return. Two weeks later, he met Daniel in the Lion's Den at the Nationals in Kalamazoo, Michigan. But this time he slew the dragon. Inside. He reached the quarterfinals and, according to Marco, he played great.

"I just decided to go out and do my best and have fun," he said. "If I lost in the first round, it would have been OK, as long as I gave it my best shot."

Step 7: Be a Role Model

You will have a lot of influence on the development of your children's character by the lessons you teach. By introducing them to youth sports and reinforcing behaviors as they participate, you contribute to their formative personality development. Your greatest impact, however, is the lessons you teach them by how you live your own life.

Children will learn how to set realistic goals and work toward meeting them if they see you doing the same thing. It is important, therefore, that you practice what you preach. Set your own goals. If you play a sport, continue to work on your own performance. Seek improvement yourself.

Your attributions regarding poor performance will also have a large impact on your child's development. When you perform poorly in tennis and blame the wind, the dead balls, or your sore elbow, you communicate a false sense of reality to your child. Do not be surprised if after the next match your son loses, he blames it on the poor line calls that his opponent made. In other words, if you do not take personal responsibilities for your own mistakes, how can you expect your children to do the same?

If you keep yourself in good physical condition, live a healthy lifestyle, and keep working toward self-improvement, your children will have a good model to emulate.

This completes our journey to the Enabler's circle. Youth sports afford many opportunities for closeness, fun, and learning about life. Enjoy your children as they participate in sports. If you keep the proper balance and follow the guidelines presented in these steps, you will experience those special moments on the sidelines.

Most of all, remember to have fun.

REFERENCES

Armstrong, Hubert. "Parenting the Elite Athlete." *Puget Soundings* (February 1986), pp. 6–9.

Bloom, Benjamin, ed. *Developing Talent in Young People.* New York: Ballantine, 1985.

Hellstedt, Jon. "Family Characteristics of Ski Racers." Unpublished paper, 1986.

Loehr, Jim. "The Pressure Cooker: One Case Study." *World Tennis* (October 1986), pp. 12–13.

Martens, Rainer. *The Joy and Sadness in Children's Sports.* Champaign, Ill.: Human Kinetics, 1978.

Orlick, Terry. *In Pursuit of Excellence.* Champaign, Ill.: Human Kinetics, 1980.

Tharp, Roland, and Ronald Gallimore. "What a Coach Can Teach a Teacher." *Psychology Today* (January 1976), pp. 75–78.

Chapter 5

Fundamentals of Conditioning

by Daniels S. Rooks, M.S.

You are now entering the final leg of your journey through this book. Throughout the next two chapters we will work together to understand and apply many of the basic principles of conditioning. Along the way, we will examine several fundamentals that are used by successful professional and amateur athletes to improve their physical condition or to "get in shape" for their sport.

Before getting into conditioning and training for your child, let's review the general physical condition of children in the United States. People are under the false impression that most children today are in better physical condition compared to when their parents were children. The truth is that the general trend of the fitness of children in the United States has steadily declined over the past forty years. Suggested causes of this decline include increased time spent at sedentary activities such as watching television and playing video and computer games. Even with the increase in children's involvement in organized sports activities, the majority of children in the United States are in unsatisfactory physical condition.

Today children have a greater opportunity to be in better physical condition than children had twenty years ago. Home fitness equipment and increased sports organizations for young children all contribute to this improved opportunity. It is important not only to get a child involved in physical fitness activities but to ensure that they learn how to participate safely. This practice will allow the child the greatest opportunity to enjoy his or her involvement in sports.

Where the general childhood population is becoming less physically fit, the opposite is happening to the competitive athlete. Athletes are becoming faster, larger, and more skillful than their prior competitors. Looking at the world record books will verify this fact. This enhancement of size, speed, and skill is occurring at a younger age as well. Some of the reasons behind these advances stem from improvements in coaching techniques, diet, psychological support, and increased levels of physical condition (fitness).

Ahead we will focus our attention on the issues of weight training and flexibility and their contribution to the development of improved physical fitness. We will examine in detail the different aspects of a safe and effective weight training program. In this chapter we will review some fundamental physiology and apply that information to support the truths and dispel the myths about weight training for the child athlete.

THE PURPOSE OF CONDITIONING

Does every child need a conditioning program?

Not every child who participates in organized sports needs a conditioning program. The objective of a conditioning program is to improve the athlete's physical condition. By being more physically fit, the performance of sport skills are often made easier. If a specific skill can be performed with less physical effort, more attention can be placed on proper technique. With improved technique the skill is usually more successfully performed. When children begin to succeed at the skills of a sport, they usually enjoy themselves more. As well, muscles and bones that have been conditioned are stronger. Stronger muscles and bones are better able to withstand the normal bumps and bruises that accompany sports participation.

What makes a good conditioning program?

There are four components to a conditioning program: muscle strength, muscle endurance, muscle and joint flexibility, and cardiovascular or aerobic fitness. It is quite common for athletes involved in a conditioning program to concentrate on only one or two of these components. For example, it is tempting for a football player to concentrate on muscle strength and neglect flexibility. It is common for a gymnast to focus on flexibility and neglect aerobic training. As a parent you can help prevent such a pitfall by encouraging a total conditioning program. (Later in this chapter we will examine the parent's role in assisting the child in a safe and effective conditioning program.)

How can improved strength and flexibility help my child?

The two most important benefits of enhanced strength and flexibility to the young athlete are the improvement of performance and the reduction in the number of injuries.

Increased muscle strength allows the muscle to generate a greater amount of force through the muscle's full range of motion. In the athlete increased strength can be seen when a figure skater has more height in his or her jumps; a gymnast continues to pull or push himself or herself more easily for a longer routine; a tennis player moves to the ball quicker and has greater power in his or her ground strokes; an ice hockey player shoots the puck harder and faster; a baseball player hits the ball farther; a softball player throws the ball farther and faster.

Increasing one's ability to produce and sustain force enables the athlete to potentially perform given tasks such as running, throwing, shooting, swimming, and jumping faster or farther than he or she could before. This concept is the basis for the attention now being placed on preseason training or "getting in shape" for a particular sport. The importance and success of conditioning is evidenced over the past ten to fifteen years by the presence of strength and conditioning coaches on the staffs of every professional and major college football team. This staff position is also present in many other professional and amateur (Olympic and college) sports including baseball, basketball, hockey, wrestling, swimming, and gymnastics. In addition, teams are undergoing fitness evaluations as part of their preseason program and are being given exercise and conditioning programs to maintain their fitness levels in the off-season.

Improving flexibility is one of the best ways to help reduce the chance of injury or its severity, particularly muscle strains or pulls. Strength without flexibility limits performance. Contrary to popular myth, a weight training program emphasizing the performance of exercises through a full range of motion, develops muscle strength *and* flexibility. Optimal flexibility, however, is not developed strictly through the performance of weight-training exercises. It is essential to include appropriate stretching or flexibility exercises as part of the conditioning program.

When one performs an athletic task, the muscle can be unexpectedly overstretched. Depending on the length the muscle is stretched, the flexibility developed by a proper weight training and stretching program will prevent or reduce the injury. If muscles and the surrounding structures are stronger and more flexible, the chance of stretch-type injuries to muscles, tendons, and ligaments is reduced. Groin muscle injuries are common in soccer players. These injuries are often caused when one foot is firmly planted and the other is forcibly stretched to the side. This injury can occur while trying to steal or block the ball from an opponent. The forced separation of the legs causes an overstretching of the muscles in the upper inner thigh, which can result in a muscle injury known as a strain or pull. If the athlete's muscles were able to stretch the greater distance comfortably, minimal or no injury would occur.

With the great increase in children's participation in organized sports, greater physical and emotional demands are being placed on young people today. These demands must be buffered by adequate preparation so that children can safely enjoy sports involvement.

TERMINOLOGY

Before getting into the principles of weight training and conditioning, let's review some of the terminology we will be using.

What do the terms *in shape, fit,* and *conditioning* mean?

Someone who is in shape or fit has a physically sound body that is properly prepared to meet the physical demands of sports participation. This physical state is developed through the process we call conditioning. When you are fit, your body works more efficiently than when you are not. This increased efficiency is seen throughout the athlete's body, especially the heart and muscles.

When an athlete has conditioned his or her muscles to have greater flexibility and strength, movements such as running, jumping, and reaching may become faster and stronger. When a freshman enters a college football program he is usually tested to assess his current level of fitness, including strength, speed, and agility. After participating in the team's conditioning program, each player is usually retested on a yearly basis. Statistics from schools such as the University of Michigan and the University of Nebraska show dramatic improvements in their athletes' fitness. These improvements are usually seen on the football field. At the University of Nebraska, center Dave Rimington arrived as a six-foot-three freshman. That year at a weight of 235 pounds he had a vertical jump of 25 inches, bench pressed 340 pounds, and ran the 40-yard dash in 5.23 seconds. After participating in the football team's weight training and conditioning program, Dave graduated weighing 292 pounds, having a 29-inch vertical jump, bench pressing 435 pounds, and running the 40-yard dash in 5.1 seconds. Dave is a larger-than-life example. These types of changes in strength and speed are not limited to only big people. Anyone, any size, can improve his or her strength, speed, and agility with proper conditioning.

Through proper cardiovascular conditioning, the heart becomes more efficient. When the heart becomes aerobically conditioned it can pump a greater amount of blood with each beat. The heart pumps (beats) fewer times per minute. This adaptation explains why an athlete usually has a lower pulse (heart rate) than does a nonathlete. During exercise a similar situation occurs. As you exercise, the muscles require a greater amount of oxygen to work. Since oxygen is carried in the blood, and the blood is already holding most of the oxygen it can, the heart must get more blood to the muscles. The need is usually accomplished by increasing the heart rate (pulse). See for yourself by taking your pulse at the bottom of the stairs and then again after running up and down them several times.

The conditioned athlete's muscles can absorb more oxygen from the blood than can the muscles of a nonconditioned individual. Because the conditioned muscles are more efficient at taking oxygen from the blood, the conditioned athlete does not have to increase his or her heart rate as much as does the nonconditioned individual. While performing the exact same physical task, therefore, the conditioned athlete is able to perform the task with less effort. By exerting less effort you are usually able to perform better and for a longer period of time.

What do *range of motion* and *comfort range* mean?

The distance that exists without pain between the extreme shortened and lengthened positions of a muscle is called the muscle's comfort range. The joint that the muscle is acting on moves through this distance along with the muscle. The distance the joint moves is called its range of motion. One of the reasons why a joint is not able to move freely through its complete range of motion is that the muscles and tendons that cross over the joint are shortened or tight. If you do not constantly move or exercise through a joint's (muscle's) full range of motion, the muscles and tendons can actually shorten.

What is *strength?*

Strength is the greatest amount of force produced by a muscle. Running and jumping are two of the most common uses of muscle strength in sports. Increased strength is the ability to produce a greater amount of force or a high level of force repeatedly (greater number of repetitions). Increased strength results in the ability to move a heavier object or to move a lighter object through the range of motion faster.

What is *muscle endurance?*

Muscle endurance is the ability of the muscle to contract (produce force) for a longer period of time without becoming tired (fatigued). Since

Figure 5.1 Elbow range of motion.

most sports are made up of specific physical tasks such as running, jumping, pushing, and pulling, muscle endurance will allow the conditioned athlete to continue to perform those specific tasks for a longer period of time before requiring rest.

What is *flexibility*?

Flexibility refers to the ability of a muscle or group of muscles and the joint of the body the muscles act on, to move comfortably through the joint's full range of motion. When developing flexibility, movement through the range of motion should be done without excessive effort or force (no pulling or pushing). If a muscle is strong but can not move freely through a comfortable range of motion, the benefits of being strong are greatly reduced. Flexibility training is one of the key components of any conditioning program. It is one of the areas that play a major role in the prevention of muscle injuries.

What is *cardiovascular* or *aerobic fitness*?

Your body requires oxygen to function. Through training you can improve your body's efficiency in the way it uses oxygen. Moderately intensive rhythmic activities such as long-distance running, cross-country skiing, and long-distance swimming require a large amount of oxygen, primarily because the activity continues for an extended period of time (greater than four or five minutes). The aerobically conditioned athlete is able to continue a less intense pace for a longer period of time (run farther) or an increased pace for a greater amount of time than before conditioning.

In sports that require quick, all-out bursts of activity, such as hockey, tennis, gymnastics, and sprinting, aerobic conditioning will allow the athlete to recover faster between intense bouts of activity. During a hockey game the player who is aerobically fit will be better able to give 100 percent during each shift because he or she will recover faster between shifts. The player who is aerobically fit is also fresher and less tired at the end of the game or match.

What are *positive* and *negative muscle contractions?*

When a muscle contracts through its comfort range, it goes from a completely lengthened position to a completely shortened position or vice versa, and then back to the starting length. The shortening of the muscle while it is contracting is called a concentric or positive contraction. To return to the fully lengthened position the muscle lengthens while it is contracting. This event is called an eccentric or negative contraction.

A greater amount of force can be produced by the muscle that is contracting eccentrically. This action is seen in long-distance runners who have conditioned themselves on straightaways and running up hills. When they run a race that includes several long or steep sections that go down hill, however, the runners will probably feel muscle soreness in the quadriceps (muscles in the front of the thighs) the following day. While running down hill the runner's quadriceps lengthen as they contract to ''decelerate'' the runner and prevent him or her from falling.

What are the differences between *weight training,* *weight lifting,* and *strength training?*

At this point, it is important to clarify the difference between weight lifting and weight training. Weight lifting and weight training are often incorrectly used to mean the same thing. *Weight training* is a method of physical conditioning, involving the use of weight (resistance) equipment, enabling an individual to perform numerous repetitions of an exercise correctly. *Weight lifting* is defined as a sport in which a participant attempts to lift the greatest amount of weight possible one time (one repetition). Olympic and power lifting are the two weight-lifting sports in which points are collected by successfully performing three lifts. *Strength training* is any activity involving exercises that increase an individual's muscle strength.

Weight training is the only activity involving weights (or resistance equipment) that is suitable for children and young athletes. Weight lifting should not be encouraged until the child is well past puberty and has been weight training an adequate amount of time to develop the necessary foundation strength.

What is a *repetition?*

The word *repetition* in weight-training language means the performance of an exercise one time. Example: Betsy performed ten repetitions on the bench press.

What is a *set?*

A set is any number of repetitions performed in a row without an extended period of rest. Example: Jeff did three sets of ten repetitions of the squat exercise.

PRINCIPLES OF CONDITIONING

You do not have to be a scientist to understand conditioning. To understand how and why strengthening muscles through weight training is beneficial, a brief review of muscle structure and function is appropriate. The following section may serve as a refresher for those of you who are familiar with muscle anatomy and physiology. For those who have not been exposed to these areas, do not let the terminology bother you. Throughout the chapter terms and ideas will be constantly repeated and explained.

Is there more than one kind of muscle in our body?

Yes. There are three types of muscle in the human body: cardiac, smooth, and skeletal. The muscle that composes the heart is called cardiac (heart) muscle. Its appearance and enzyme concentrations differ from those of the other two types of muscle. The walls of the stomach, intestines, and arteries contain smooth muscle. Smooth muscle is also referred to as involuntary muscle because it can not be consciously controlled to contract or relax. The final class of muscle is skeletal or striated muscle. Its major function is to contract, or shorten, pulling on the bones of the skeleton to which they are attached. This pulling enables us to move. (In this book we will concentrate on skeletal muscle.)

What are *fast twitch* and *slow twitch muscle fibers?*

Muscles are composed of muscle cells or fibers. Every muscle fiber is not the same. The two major fiber types within a muscle are fast twitch and slow twitch. There are several differences between these two fiber types. One difference is the concentration of particular enzymes located within the muscle cell.

The slow twitch fiber contains enzymes that allow the utilization of oxygen and fat as energy sources. Slow twitch fibers are utilized primarily during less intense repetitive movements over an extended period of time. Examples of activities that rely heavily on slow twitch fibers include long-distance running, swimming, rowing, cycling, and cross-country skiing.

A fast twitch fiber contains a higher concentration of enzymes that allow the muscle fiber to use carbohydrate (sugar) and stored animal starch (glycogen) as their primary energy source. Fast twitch fibers are most important to the athlete who participates in activities that require rapid, explosive body movements such as sprinting, jumping, reaching, pushing, and pulling. Such activities include figure skating, gymnastics, swimming (sprinting), hockey, track, basketball, volleyball, football, baseball, soccer, judo, and karate.

One of the ways to differentiate between the two fiber types is the time it takes for a muscle to go from a relaxed state to maximal (100 percent) contraction. As you might imagine, the fast twitch muscle fiber reaction takes less time than the slow twitch muscle fiber reaction.

How can I tell if my child's muscles are primarily fast twitch or slow twitch?

A muscle biopsy is the only way of approximating the percentage of slow twitch and fast twitch fibers in a muscle. A muscle biopsy is a procedure in which through a small incision a large needle is inserted into a single muscle and a little piece of muscle is removed. This piece of muscle is treated with certain procedures that allow microscopic identification of muscle fiber types.

A muscle biopsy is an estimate of the percentage of fast and slow twitch fibers in one section of a single muscle. Since sport skills require the use of many muscles at the same time, estimating the composition of one muscle does not provide any useful information. Because of the possible health risk, parents should *not* allow a muscle biopsy to be performed on their child.

Is it important for me to know if my child's muscles are mostly fast twitch or slow twitch?

No. Everyone has muscles that are made up of both fast twitch and slow twitch muscle fibers. Most of us have approximately 50 percent of each muscle fiber type in the majority of our muscles. Children should focus their attention on developing perfect technique in the specific skills of their chosen sports. Olympic and professional athletes have successfully competed for years without knowledge of their percentage of fast and slow twitch muscle fibers.

Is exercise the only important component in the development of strength and optimal physical condition?

No. There are three major components to gaining strength and improving an athlete's physical (and mental) conditioning: proper exercise, proper diet, and proper rest. A parent can help his or her athletic child make good decisions about each of these three components. If one of the three components is left out or ignored, physical condition, performance, growth, and general health can be compromised.

About the athlete's diet, for further information you should seek the advice of a dietitian or qualified nutritionist. Currently, anyone can call himself or herself a nutritionist regardless of educational background. Make sure that the person who gives you nutrition information is qualified to do so. The individual should have a college degree in the field of human nutrition and experience dealing with individual diet consultation. Most often the nutritionist/dietitian has the initials R.D. after his or her name, indicating that person's achievement of national certification as a registered dietitian in the field of human nutrition.

For most people the newsstand magazines covering weight lifting, bodybuilding, and health and fitness are the usual sources of information. Beware of fad diet programs that boast miraculous results and success. Fundamental guidelines for good nutrition are included in the old faithful, four basic food groups: milk and dairy products, including milk, yogurt, ice cream, and cheese; meats and high protein foods, including fish, poultry, beef, and lamb; grains and breads, including wheat, rice, oatmeal, corn, and barley; and fruits and vegetables, including apples, oranges, melons, lettuce, carrots, cucumbers, and squash.

Can my child get all the nutrition he or she needs by eating regular foods, or do I need to give some sort of supplement?

Proper nutrition can be achieved by the proper selection and consumption from the four basic food groups. Supplementation is rarely necessary. A vitamin can be given if the athlete does not eat adequately. If your child eats a balanced diet, vitamins are not needed. Items such as the weight-gain protein powders are a waste of time and money. Additional protein can be taken into the body by eating a second tuna fish sandwich, for example, or replacing the afternoon cookies with a scoop of cottage cheese and some fruit. When eating that additional sandwich or substituted snack, you get not only high-quality protein but additional vitamins, minerals, and fiber as well.

What type of food is best for a pregame meal?

Traditionally, steak and eggs have been the pregame meal choice for many athletes. Research has unquestionably shown, however, that meals high in fat and protein and low in carbohydrates, such as steak and eggs, are poor choices. Fat and protein take longer to digest, which can cause the athlete to have that heavy or full feeling. Also, this type of meal can stimulate the urge to defecate. This feeling can be a problem during a competition, causing physical and psychological discomfort to the athlete.

Foods high in complex carbohydrates (starches) are best for the pregame menu. The night before a competition, a dinner of spaghetti, sauce, and bread provides the right kind of fuel. A choice of cereal, pancakes, waffles, or toast with jam for the light morning meal should be eaten three to four hours before the start of any athletic event.

At every meal fluids should be consumed. Special attention should be paid to fluid consumption during the hotter times of the year, when more is required. Eat light to moderate amounts of foods high in complex carbohydrates, and drink plenty of fluids to fuel up the morning of the big day.

Does the young athlete need high levels of protein in his or her diet?

No. In general, Americans eat more protein than necessary. As a child grows, he or she will need more protein than the adult. Most children, however, eat more than enough protein in their diets. To add more protein to an already balanced diet is not necessary. If the child does not eat a balanced diet, however, an effort of eating more fish, poultry, dairy products, beans/legumes, lean red meat, peanut butter, etc., should be made. Regardless of whether a child needs additional protein in his or her diet, foods should be used to provide that protein, and supplements such as protein powders should be avoided.

Are vitamin and mineral supplements necessary for a young athlete?

No. If the young athlete eats a balanced diet, no supplementation is necessary. Taking high (mega) doses of the fat-soluble vitamins (A, D, E, and K) can produce toxic effects. Excessive amounts of vitamins or minerals do not improve an athlete's performance. For a female who exercises vigorously and has a heavy menstral blood flow, an iron supplement may be considered. If your daughter is in this category, you should consult a physician for recommendations.

Should my child take salt pills?

Most athletes do not sweat enough to warrant the use of salt pills. Salt is found in almost all processed foods and is usually consumed in sufficient quantities to replenish any amount of salt lost through sweating. If the athlete is involved in vigorous activity during the summer or in any hot environment, the addition of the salt shaker at the table or a handful or two of potato chips is usually sufficient to replenish what is needed.

If salt pills are taken for some reason, they should never be taken immediately before the athletic activity. The high concentration of salt in the stomach and intestine will force the body to pull water into the intestine to dilute the tablet, which leaves a smaller amount of water available for the many other vital bodily functions taking place.

How much sleep should my child get each night?

Muscle does not grow and become stronger while it is being exercised. It grows while it recovers, and the best time for recovery is while a person sleeps.

Some children require more sleep, others less. Some children seem to sleep through puberty, and their parents figure they will be about eight feet tall when they are through growing. Others seem to survive adequately on only six to seven hours of sleep. For a child involved in a conditioning program, eight to ten hours of sleep per night is not uncommon.

If your child is tired, lethargic, or seems to be doing poorly in practice or competition, he or she may be worn out. You will often have to intervene and provide the child the opportunity to get more sleep. Sleep, of course, should not excuse one from cleaning up one's room or helping around the house.

What is a *warm-up*, and is it necessary for all sports?

Warm-up refers to a sequence of activities or exercises that are performed before beginning a more strenuous physical activity or exercise. The topic of warm-up has been controversial for many years. Several individuals feel warm-up does not improve athletic performance and may not be of any physiological benefit. The vast majority of knowledgeable people in exercise physiology and sports medicine, however, feel that a warm-up period is essential for both children and adults prior to participating in all sports activities.

How is warm-up beneficial in improving performance and reducing the chance of injury?

Warm-up increases the amount of blood flowing to the muscles and surrounding structures. This acceleration in blood flow raises the temperature of the muscles. As a result, the amount of force and speed a muscle is capable of generating also increases. The higher temperature also enhances the pliability of muscles, tendons, and ligaments. This increased pliability allows the joint's range of motion and the muscle's comfort range to increase, thereby reducing the chance of an overstretching-type of injury.

What is a *cool-down* and why is it important?

A cool-down is the performance of several slow rhythmic exercises immediately following an activity. A cool-down allows the body's systems that were affected by exercise to return gradually to normal. Heart rate, breathing rate, and blood flow to the active muscles, for example, are all elevated during the exercise period. During the cool-down they begin to decrease and return to resting (before exercise) levels.

The importance of the cool-down period is seen in the sprinter or distance runner who has had a tremendous amount of blood sent to the muscles of the legs during exercise. Without the muscles' constant movement after the event, such as walking, gravity causes a great quantity of blood to pool in the veins of the legs, which is why one should never sit down immediately after running. This buildup reduces the total amount of blood available for the brain and the rest of the body, and the runner might pass out.

A cool-down can be as simple as walking several hundred yards after a foot race or pedaling or swimming with little effort in order to continue working the exercising muscles. During easy, smooth, nonstressful activities, the muscles actually squeeze the veins, causing the blood to return to the heart.

After exercise the muscles of the body are more pliable. The performance of flexibility exercises during this period allows the child to stretch further than usual. This can develop both musculoskeletal flexibility and a child's positive attitude towards stretching. Two or three stretching exercises, usually the exercises the child finds most troublesome, should be included as part of the cool-down.

What is *isometric exercise?*

The word *isometrics* can be broken up into two parts. *Iso* means "the same" or "unchanged," and *metrics* means "length." Therefore, isometric exercise is done by applying a resistance such that the muscle being exercised does not change in length. With isometrics there is no range of motion. The joint or joints the muscles act on do not move.

What is *dynamic exercise?*

Dynamics means that the limb and muscle are moving during the performance of the exercise. *Isotonics*, which means the same *(iso)* weight or resistance *(tonics)*, was the term that used to be used to describe dynamics.

Dynamics is subdivided into three main areas: constant resistance, variable resistance, and accommodating resistance. Constant resistance involves the use of equipment (free weights, most single and multistation machines) that supplies a *constant* (the same) resistance throughout the entire range of action. Accommodating resistance, or isokinetics, involves expensive high-tech equipment that controls the *speed* at which the limb can move.

Variable resistance refers to specially designed machines or other pieces of equipment that change the resistance at points through the range of action. Variable resistance equipment (Nautilus, special multistation machines, nonweight items) is built on the principle that as the muscle moves through its range of motion there is a position (muscle length) at which the muscle is stronger. The machine increases the resistance at the points of the range of motion where the muscle is stronger and reduces the resistance at the points where the muscle is not as strong. This type of machine allows the muscle to be exercised with greater intensity.

Isokinetic equipment is used to measure muscle strength and endurance by most hospitals, sports medicine facilities, and extensive athletic programs at the college, Olympic, and professional levels. Because of the large expense involved with the isokinetic machines, these items will not be considered for your child's conditioning program.

METHODS OF EXERCISE

There are many different muscle-conditioning programs on the market today. However, they all fall under three basic technique categories of resistance training: using the individual's own body (calisthenics, isometrics); using weighted (i.e., free-weight) equipment specifically designed to supply a resistance to muscles while performing specific exercises; and using nonweighted equipment (i.e., surgical tubing, springs).

In this section we will examine these three types of exercise for strengthening muscles. We will look at the pros and cons of each method from the child athlete's point of view of strength-developing potential, cost, safety, and benefits for sport conditioning.

Calisthenics. Calisthenics utilizes a person's own body weight and gravity to supply resistance to the muscle. Requiring minimal or no equipment, this type of conditioning is safe and effective for the child who is beginning a conditioning program and who does not wish to get involved in weight training. Calisthenics can also be used to supplement an ongoing conditioning program.

The athlete must use common sense, and remember always to be in control of his or her body movements. Strength development can range from fair to very good, depending on the athlete's persistence and the specific exercises performed. Common calisthenic exercises include push-ups, pull-ups, sit-ups, dips, squat leaps, and jumping jacks.

Isometrics. Isometrics can be used to maintain or moderately improve muscle tone and strength. Very young athletes or those individuals who are recovering from an injury or surgery can most effectively use isometrics. No equipment is required. Therefore, there is virtually no cost involved.

The time needed for an isometric workout depends on the number of muscles exercised, and is shorter than a conventional workout. To perform isometric exercises you can use any immovable object such as a door frame, wall, or even the nonexercising hand or leg. The muscle should be exercised at several different lengths (figure 5.2) during the workout. Contract the muscle as hard as you can by pushing or pulling on the object for six to ten seconds. Each exercise can be repeated one or more times, but usually not more than four.

The major problem with isometrics is that the athlete does not gain strength throughout the muscle's full range of motion. Because the muscle and joint do not move, strength is virtually limited to the length of

Figure 5.2 Biceps exercise at flexed, middle, and extended positions.

the muscle at which it is exercised. With isometrics no improvement is seen in flexibility. Therefore, it is essential to include flexibility exercises with an isometric program.

If isometrics is the only method of exercise performed, motivation can become a problem. Without movement of a weight or other object there is no immediate feedback. Increasing the amount of weight one can lift or the number of repetitions one can perform is the type of positive feedback young people need to keep them excited about conditioning.

For young children isometrics can be an adequate form of exercise as long as flexibility exercises are included. Young children may find this program to be a sufficient method of muscle strengthening but eventually will probably become bored. Isometrics is fast, inexpensive, convenient, and does not require much preparation.

Free Weights. Free-weight exercise is the oldest method of developing strength. Lifting an object of constant weight goes back before Greek and Roman times, when men lifted heavy objects such as rocks and animals to get stronger. Times have changed, and the equipment is easier to find and use, and does not require feeding. Most of all, the cost of free-weight equipment is reasonable, much less than that needed to purchase the equivalent machines to provide an equal variety of exercises.

Free weights include barbells, dumbbells, and other pieces of equipment that allow a constant weight to be moved freely, without restriction. This method of exercise differs from a machine by requiring the athlete to balance the weight using additional muscles (secondary) to those being worked by the exercise (primary). The equipment is characterized by plates that can be put on or taken off a bar to vary the resistance. Some equipment, however, can not be adjusted but can still be used in a free-weight program. Cast iron or plastic dumbbells, for example, are just as effective as the adjustable type but are limited in their use, because the weight (resistance) can not be increased as the athlete becomes stronger.

Free weights enable an athlete to perform freestanding exercises that require the use of additional "stabilizer" muscles to balance and support the weight through its movement. This balance and stabilization required of free weights strengthens a greater number of muscles, tendons, and ligaments, giving improved stability to joints. In addition, increased demands on contraction, stabilization, and balance contribute to neuromuscular coordination. Some athletes seem to have a better ability to control their movements, their balance, and their eye-hand coordination. This difference is primarily due to integration between the nerve and the muscles it innervates. Conditioning will not create a "natural" athlete, but it will assist in developing better communication between the nerves and the muscles they innervate.

With a barbell and two adjustable-weight dumbbells one can perform an unlimited number of exercises. These exercises work all of the major muscle groups in the body. Both concentric and eccentric contractions can be performed on this equipment.

Safety is an important concern in the use of free weights. The athlete should pay particular attention to the proper technique of each exercise and not try to lift more weight than he or she is able to. Always have someone monitor the training sessions and be available to assist the athlete in completing the final repetition of an exercise if necessary. When tired, the athlete should stop weight training and return when better rested (same day or following day). A tired athlete often lacks the concentration necessary to perform an exercise safely. (The finer points of safety, as they relate to specific weight training exercises, are discussed in the next chapter.)

Machines. Today there are a multitude of exercise machines on the market. Exercise machines are much more accessible to young athletes (both competitive and noncompetitive) than they were twenty years ago, due to the increase in fitness awareness both at home and in the schools. They are a safe and effective method of weight training. The majority of high schools and possibly junior high schools now have at least one multistation machine. Home fitness machines are also very popular. Most multistation machines allow the athlete to perform exercises for each of the major muscle areas of the body.

The strength-developing capability of the majority of weight training machines is equal to that of free weights at a beginning and intermediate level. For the majority of individuals, cost is the primary reason for not choosing a weight training machine for the child weight trainer. With the large number of machines presently on the market, the cost should continue to drop and eventually stabilize.

Safety is an important factor when considering a weight training machine. For the young athlete who will not have constant supervision while weight training, a machine is an important consideration.

Nonweight Equipment. Use of nonweight equipment to supply resistance is a common practice in several sports. An item such as surgical tubing, an inner tube, or a spring-type device can be used. The amount and kind of resistance supplied to the muscles depends on the material the device is made of. In judo an inner tube can supply resistance to develop one's strength in the throwing skills. In ice hockey an inner tube or surgical tubing tied around an athlete's waist and secured to the boards can strengthen leg muscles and improve endurance. After the muscle becomes stronger, the child will be able to pull the tubing or spring farther and faster than before.

The cost of nonweight equipment training is nominal. If you have an old bicycle tire with an inner tube in it, you are ahead of the game. If you can not find an inner tube at a bicycle store, try surgical tubing, which can be purchased at most hospital supply stores, drug stores, and apothecaries. Other pieces of equipment such as springs can be purchased at stores that have a large sporting-goods department.

Most of the nonweight items are safe for the young athlete. When using the springs that you pull apart, he or she should be careful to keep the spring away from the skin. A black-and-blue mark (from pinching) in the shape of short vertical lines may be left behind. Stretchy items such as inner tubes and surgical tubing can snap if accidentally let go. Being conscious of this fact usually is all that is needed to prevent an accident.

Another type of nonweight resistance equipment is that which uses air (e.g., shock absorbers) or water to supply the resistance to the muscle. Several new pieces of equipment are currently on the market. Most of these, however, are too costly to be considered for home use. If you belong to a fitness or health club that has such equipment, be sure to get the advice of a qualified instructor before trying them.

What is the best way to develop strength?

A muscle increases in strength responding to overload. Overload occurs when greater demands are placed on the muscle. Weight training or resistance training is the best method for supplying a muscle with the overload necessary to develop muscle strength. Strength increases when you ask a muscle to work harder than it normally does during daily activities. To develop strength (the response) you have to apply resistance (the stimulus). The resistance, in this case a weight, causes the muscle to grow and adapt to the increased demand being asked of it (conditioning). Strength increases in response to this demand and adaptation is seen as an increase in the muscle's size and strength. As the muscle adapts and becomes stronger, the weight (resistance) is easier to lift. To continue to develop strength, resistance (weight) is continuously added in small increments. One of the biggest mistakes people make is to move up in weight (increase the resistance) too soon and by too much. When this happens, technique suffers and the body can not adapt (grow) properly. The athlete must increase the weight only when his or her body is ready. (We will discuss the correct method of increasing the resistance in the following chapter.)

Is it worthwhile for my child to weight train?

Yes. Until recently, physicians and scientists felt it was not possible for the young child to develop strength through weight training. Based on current research, it has been shown that children who have not yet reached puberty as well as children who have passed puberty are able to increase muscle strength by participating in a weight-training program. How much strength and muscle size is developed depends on several factors. Children who have not yet reached puberty will not develop muscle size and strength as fast or to the same extent as children who have begun or passed puberty. Also, boys will develop muscle size and strength faster and to a greater extent than girls.

Is it safe for a child to weight train?

Yes. This is a question often asked by both parents and coaches. Weight training safety at any age is based primarily on the weight trainer's (and spotter's) knowledge of correct exercise technique and his or her attention to performing that technique properly. Regardless of the athlete's age, the first objective of the weight training instructor or coach should be to teach the correct technique of each exercise. Beyond the safety factor, performing the proper technique allows the athlete to exercise optimally the muscle or muscles he or she wishes to develop. If the athlete is going to spend the time weight training, why not get the most out of the effort? Improper technique does not exercise the muscle to the best advantage and can lead to injury. Attention to safety should always be observed by anyone who weight trains.

A child should ideally begin weight training under the guidance of a parent or coach who is knowledgeable and experienced in proper exercise technique. (If you are not experienced in weight training techniques, do not be discouraged. In the following chapter each exercise is described in detail to allow parents who are not familiar with weight training to coach themselves and their child through each of the exercises.) Regardless of your level of experience, your first priority as a weight training coach should be always to stress correct form and not the maximal amount of weight the athlete is able to lift. Under these circumstances weight training can be a safe, productive, and enjoyable activity for the child, and for you the parent.

Another important consideration for the parent is the quality of weight training equipment to be used. Types of equipment will be described and discussed throughout these two chapters.

What is the appropriate age to begin weight training?

With young people trying to become better athletes at a younger age, it is important for a parent to identify and encourage the proper avenues to pursue, and potential hazards to avoid. Each young athlete should be considered individually in one of the following groups. Table 5.1 defines safe limits.

The number of repetitions recommended is a range that includes the maximum and minimum number of repetitions in each set. The higher the number of repetitions, the more muscle endurance is stressed, whereas the lower the number of repetitions, the more strength development is stressed.

Table 5.1.   Safe weight training program.

| | Regimen by Age Group | | |
	1	2	3
Exercises per body part	1	2	>2
Sets	1-2	2-4	3-6
Repetitions	12-15	10-12	6-10
Maximum weight used	very light	moderate	heavy

Before Puberty (Group 1). The first group includes children who have not yet reached puberty. These young children must be handled with care to ensure that no physiological damage occurs through overtraining. Weight training will bring about small improvements in strength and muscle size. The athlete's aim should be to improve muscle tone and introduce his or her body to proper exercise technique. Children in this age group should perform one or two sets, with twelve to fifteen repetitions per set, using only very light weights.

Early Adolescence (Group 2). During early adolescence, from puberty to sixteen years of age, children are developing both physically and emotionally. This age group can perform three or four sets of ten to twelve repetitions per set using moderate resistance. *Moderate resistance* is defined as a weight the athlete can control for a minimum of ten repetitions without resting.

Young Adulthood (Group 3). The last age group includes athletes from seventeen to twenty-one years of age. At this stage the athlete who has been participating in a weight training program and has developed the strength and coordination necessary to perform the exercises properly may now begin to handle heavier weights, fewer repetitions (six to ten per set), and more sets (three to six) per exercise. However, if a person has not been weight training properly prior to becoming seventeen years old, he or she should begin to train using the early adolescent schedule until proper exercise form and adequate strength have been established.

Will my child become "muscle bound" from weight training?

No. *Muscle boundness*, a term frequently used about ten years ago but less so today, refers to a tightness or restriction of movement thought to be brought about by the increase in muscle size produced by weight training. Today someone who is thought to be muscle bound is now called tight or inflexible.

Children often show a lack of flexibility. As a child's bones grow lengthwise, the muscles that cover them are stretched like rubber bands. As you pull the two ends of a rubber band away from each other, the remaining length it is able to stretch comfortably is reduced. Once stretched, the amount of tension in the rubber band increases as it is lengthened. This elasticity is what occurs in the growing athlete as his or her muscles are being stretched as the bones they are attached to lengthen. Some children's muscles adapt to this stretching (growing) faster than others. Flexibility exercises will help minimize the reduction in flexibility seen with growth. The most critical time is during the rapid spurts of growth that occur at puberty.

Not performing weight training exercises throughout the muscle's full range of motion can cause inflexibility. Improper technique is often used to make an exercise easier to perform (because a muscle is weakest in its lengthened or fully stretched position). If a person does not stretch his or her muscles to the limit periodically, the muscles will actually shorten or decrease their comfort range. Properly performed weight training exercises help maintain and develop flexibility.

BENEFITS OF WEIGHT TRAINING AND CONDITIONING

Preventive medicine is the measure or measures that should be taken to help reduce the risk factors associated with injury of any kind. One of the most important components of any health care program is preventive medicine. Currently, preventive medicine is practiced to combat tooth decay, cancer, heart disease, high blood pressure, and obesity. Most children are introduced to preventive medicine through their dentist in the association between fluoride and the reduction of cavities. The same philosophy of undergoing regular checkups and knowing what measures can be taken to reduce the chance of injury should be followed in sports participation.

In the field of sports medicine and conditioning, preventive medicine is beginning to receive greater attention. In the Division of Sports Medicine at The Children's Hospital in Boston, for example, a program called CHAMPS (Children's Hospital Athletic Medicine Preventive Screening) evaluates young athletes between seven and twenty-one years of age. Each athlete performs an extensive battery of painless, noninvasive tests to assess many physical characteristics. Nutritional, orthopedic, and psychological (currently under review) information is also collected. This gathering of physiological information allows a physical profile to be developed on each athlete.

The measurement information is used in part to identify any physical weaknesses that may predispose that athlete to injury. From the profile assessment an exercise prescription is developed to correct these weaknesses and to improve the athlete's overall fitness level. The purpose of the CHAMPS program is to assist the child to be better physically prepared for participation in his or her chosen sport. CHAMPS' goal is to optimize the child's enjoyment and fun in sports by reducing the incidence of injury and improving performance.

A young female tennis player came through the CHAMPS program with complaints of regularly occurring muscle strains (pulls). She is an up-and-coming tennis player whose constant injuries prevented her from playing up to her potential. She was making the transition from high school to college and was frustrated by her constant setbacks. Her evaluation showed that she was excessively tight (decreased flexibility) in several body areas and that her upper body and leg strength was low. The test results came as a surprise to both the athlete and her mother, for the athlete had been performing stretching exercises for several years. This young woman was very diligent and worked hard at complying with her exercise prescription. Her hard work paid off when she was able to compete and train for an entire summer without a muscle strain.

In order to compete at a higher level or intensity, proper physical conditioning is necessary to reduce the chance of injury and improve performance. Proper conditioning is one of the first lines of action towards preventing minor injuries, decreasing the intensity of certain major injuries, and improving an athlete's skill performance.

How can weight training help my child avoid injury?

Proper strength training for an athlete of any age can reduce the chance of minor injuries. A weight training program helps prevent muscle, tendon, and ligament injuries primarily by making these structures stronger. Through weight training the athlete strengthens muscle tissue, the tendons that attach muscles to the bones, and the ligaments that support the joint the muscles move. For example, the biceps muscle (front of the upper arm), its tendons, and the ligaments of the elbow, wrist, and shoulder joints are strengthened by performing the biceps curl. Increased strength improves the muscle's, tendons', and ligaments' ability to absorb the bumps and normal stresses that occur during sports participation. With these changes brought about through weight training, the athlete's body is better prepared to meet the physical challenge of performing the skills of a given activity or sport without being injured.

COMPARISON OF WEIGHT TRAINING EQUIPMENT FOR THE YOUNG ATHLETE

In the following section commonly asked questions dealing with different types of weight training equipment are addressed. In many cases the choice of equipment is restricted to the location where the young athlete exercises (at home, school, or a gym or health club). Each piece of equipment has its strengths and weaknesses. We will address these pros and cons from the needs of the growing athlete.

Which kind of equipment is the safest for young weight trainers?

For the beginning weight trainer, machines offer an added safety factor that is not found with free weights. Although a spotter should still be present to assist the athlete in his or her workout, the chance of injury due to a weight falling on someone is greatly reduced. With the Universal machine's bench-press exercise, for example, if the athlete is working out alone and is unable to complete the last repetition, the weight can be returned safely to the stack. With the free-weight bench-press exercise, however, one must be careful not to get caught under the bar (not being able to push the bar back up to the supports). Supervision is essential.

Figure 5.3   Bench-press machine.

Are free weights safe for beginning weight trainers?

Yes. Free weights are safe for a child of any age who is involved in a weight training program. This assurance is based on the premise that the child is old enough and strong enough to handle the minimum weight of the empty barbell or dumbbell. To use free weights a child should be able to perform a minimum of one set of fifteen repetitions of an exercise with the empty bar plus the collars.

The weights are not supported by anything except the athlete. For this reason a spotter is absolutely essential when an athlete uses free weights. If adequate supervision is not available, free weights are not recommended and machines should be used. For very young children who can not perform the necessary number of repetitions with the empty bar, a broomstick, a dowel rod, books, or other similar objects can be substituted to perform the exercises. (The following chapter contains a list of several weight training exercises that can be performed with either barbell or broomstick, dumbbell or book.) Constant supervision is still necessary regardless of whether a young child is using a barbell or broomstick.

Is one type of equipment easier to learn a proper technique on?

Learning proper weight training exercise technique is usually easier for the young athlete on a machine than with free weights. A machine is designed to move a particular distance in a predetermined path, and is therefore easier to use. The range of motion of an individual's movement is limited by the machine. The bar or handles of a machine move through the same path every repetition, providing the athlete with a better understanding of how his or her body should be positioned around the bar during the performance of the exercise. This operation prevents the weight trainer from being distracted by the need to balance or stabilize the weight, allowing for complete concentration on the technique of the exercise.

Many children will not have the opportunity to use machines to begin a weight training program. Others may just prefer to begin with free weights. In these situations free weights are an equally good method to start with. Free-weight exercises require more attention to detail than machines do, however, and therefore make the learning process a little more time-consuming. In contrast to a machine, because the path the weight travels in space is totally determined by the athlete's muscular control, the chance of incorrect technique is increased. To avoid one's learning bad habits and potentially dangerous technique, an individual who understands the proper exercise technique should be present.

For these reasons it is suggested that young children be introduced to weight training by machines if regular supervision will not be available. If proper supervision is available, which is recommended, either method can be used. Over time the athlete develops an intuitive feel for the exercise technique, and focuses on performing the number of repetitions desired instead of the correct technique. Once an athlete has become familiar with the exercise techniques and teaches his or her body "how to move" and "where to go" when performing an exercise, he or she will be better able to handle free weights safely and confidently.

Are there any differences in weight training equipment for the child and adolescent-aged athlete?

Yes. The needs and results from weight training differ between the child and adolescent. For most athletes, as their strength and weight training skills increase, the need to incorporate free weights into their strength training program also increases.

By moving in a constant path of motion, machines present a disadvantage. When the body does not use stabilizer muscles (muscles required to balance and steady the weighted bar), the total amount of muscular strength developed is less than when free weights are used. Machines provide resistance at a particular angle, depending on where the body lines up in relation to the equipment. All the athlete has to do is push or pull to perform a repetition. Because they use stabilizer muscles, free weights should eventually be incorporated into a weight training program to develop the most strength. Use of free weights also develops neuromuscular coordination, which is brought about through the stabilization and balancing of the weight during the exercise. Neuromuscular development is seen with machines, but only to a fraction of that developed with free weights. Therefore, free weights, which require balancing and stabilizing, demand a greater amount of overall body strength to perform a given repetition of the same exercise. Because more strength is required for each repetition, more total strength is developed.

What is a lifting or weight training belt, and does my child need one?

Weight training, weight lifting, and lifting belts are synonymous names for the same piece of equipment. A weight lifting belt is an extra-wide leather belt used to provide support for the lower back and abdo-

 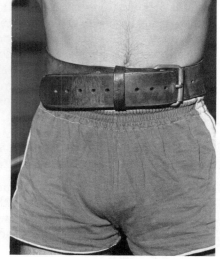

Figure 5.4   Weight training belt.

men. The belt provides a "bridge" that distributes the pressure placed on the lower back, by the motion of the exercise, to the upper back and hips. It therefore protects the more susceptible lower back and adbominal structures.

A weight training belt can measure either four or six inches high in the back and two or four inches wide in the front. The choice depends on comfort and support. The belt should be worn around the upper part of the waist, usually covering the belly button. It should be tightened to fit snugly without discomfort. When the athlete takes a deep breath, a feeling of total midsection support is felt. Because very young beginners will be using light weights, it is not essential to find a belt that will fit this age group. Special attention to proper technique will compensate in this circumstance. However, when working with children and early adolescents, a weight training belt provides an added safety factor. It does not have to be worn for every exercise. As the athlete spends more time in the weight room, a belt can be a good source of psychological as well as physical support.

Several other accessories are popular items in weight lifting magazines. It is important for parents to minimize the flash and glitter of weight training and teach their children to focus on proper technique and perseverance. A young athlete may need a particular piece of equipment, such as gloves, to provide added protection and comfort. The degree of equipment involvement is something that you and your child can discuss as the need arises.

Chapter 6

Getting to Work: The Specifics of Weight Training

by Daniel S. Rooks, M.S.

Welcome to the final step of your journey. We will now examine the specifics of a weight training program. The major emphasis of this chapter is to provide the detailed guidelines that you and your child will need to begin a weight training program. If your child is already involved in weight training, this chapter can be used to ensure that your child is performing each exercise correctly.

In chapter 5 we explored several of the physiological fundamentals of conditioning and most specifically the whys of weight training. Your understanding of why proper conditioning is important for your child is an accomplishment that separates you from the majority of parents and coaches. If you have skipped the previous chapter and come directly here, please go back and read it. If you have already read chapter 5, this is the moment you have been waiting for. Here is where we will put it all together and discuss *how* to put your knowledge to work. So, put on your shorts, a T-shirt or leotard, lace up your sneakers, and let's get to the part that is the most fun.

A complete conditioning program has several components. In this chapter we will examine the weight training and flexibility components.

It is important to remember to include aerobic or endurance-type activities in your total conditioning program. Examples of aerobic activities include running, bicycling, swimming, cross-country skiing, and jumping rope. To prevent training error and injury, begin slowly with an activity and increase approximately 5 to 10 percent every week or two. In other words, the athlete who has never run before should begin with five minutes of running and every week or two add fifteen to fifty seconds to the running time. This increase may seem like a small amount, but all aspects of conditioning are built on a solid foundation of consistent workouts and constant effort. If your child begins too fast, he or she may get hurt and have to begin again. This "yo-yo syndrome" of starting an exercise program, getting injured, resting for a period of time, and starting over is self-defeating toward the goal of optimal physical fitness and sports participation.

This chapter includes a flexibility program and beginning weight training program, both of which provide at least one exercise for each of the major muscle areas: shoulders, chest, back (including low back), abdomen, arms, and legs.

For each of these exercises there is a step-by-step description of the equipment needed, the muscles involved, the starting position, the proper technique, and safety tips. Before your child attempts any exercise, be sure you both read through the description of each exercise carefully. Talk your way through each exercise before actually trying it. For the flexibility exercises, have the athlete *slowly* move his or her body into the proper position to ensure that the correct muscles are being stretched. For the weight training exercises, have the athlete go through the motions of getting into the proper starting position and moving his or her body through the exercise without using a weight. This dry run will give you both a chance to see how each exercise should look and feel. The extra minute or so is well worth the effort.

WARM-UP

As we have seen in the previous chapter, warming up before any form of physical activity is very important. A warm-up should always be done before every weight training session and any type of sports practice or competition.

What is a good warm-up program?

A warm-up program can entail almost any form of exercise that gradually places stress on muscles and joints. A warm-up program should begin with a gentle, repetitive activity such as fast walking, an easy bicycle ride, stroking around a rink, or some similar activity. This step should be followed by two or three calisthenic activities such as jumping jacks and push-ups. Lastly, several flexibility exercises that cover the major muscle groups to be exercised should be performed. Remember, the entire warm-up should last approximately fifteen to twenty minutes. (Suggestions of exercises that may be included in a flexibility program are listed and described in great detail later in this chapter.)

What kind of warm-up is best for my child's sport?

Warm-up intensity and duration depend upon the activity to follow. If explosive muscular contractions are required, as in sprinting, swimming, football, and judo, a warm-up involving extensive flexibility is necessary. Walking, stretching, and calisthenic-type exercises are suggested. On the other hand, slow, rhythmic muscle activity such as long-distance running requires less of a warm-up. For the majority of sports that combine slow, rhythmic activity with explosive muscular contractions, a warm-up combining both extensive stretching and calisthenics is recommended. Fifteen to twenty minutes should be allotted prior to every exercise or sports training session or competition for proper warm-up.

What is the correct way to stretch?

It is not enough just to warm up. *How* we warm up is important. Warm-up and stretching exercises should be done gently and when relaxed. From the correct starting position the athlete should move his or her body until the feeling of slight tightness is felt in the areas of the body that are to be stretched. We will call this point of slight tightness the *action point*. The body is held in position at the *action point* for sixty seconds. There should be no bouncing! Slow, smooth, gentle stretching is the best way to improve flexibility. If the athlete can not hold the stretched position for sixty seconds due to pain, he or she has stretched past the *action point*. When overstretching occurs the athlete should ease back to the starting position and begin again.

Flexibility is one of the major components of fitness that people take for granted or ignore. Flexibility, however, is relatively easy to improve in most children. Stretching falls under the you-get-out-of-it-what-you-put-into-it category. The more days in a row the athlete stretches, the more improvement he or she will see. The ideal flexibility program is seven days a week.

An athlete's stretching program should include at least one flexibility exercise for each body part used in the sport. For most sports this includes exercises for the front, back, and sides of the thigh; calf; trunk; lower and upper back; arms; chest; and shoulders. The following exercises can be used as the stretching portion of a warm-up program.

WARM-UP EXERCISES

Before beginning any type of stretching program, the athlete should always perform some kind of nonstressful, total body exercise such as jumping jacks, brisk walking, or jogging for two to three minutes.

BODY AREA: Neck
EXERCISE: Head circles
PURPOSE: To stretch and warm the muscles of the neck area

Begin with arms at your side, shoulders straight, feet approximately shoulder-width apart, and eyes forward. In a slow, smooth motion begin to roll your head to the side, bringing your ear as close to your shoulder as comfortably possible, while looking straight ahead. Continue moving your head in a circular motion. When your head is rolled back your eyes should be looking up, and when your head is rolled forward your chin should be tucked close to your chest. Continue the exercise, moving first in a clockwise motion five times, then in a counterclockwise motion five times.

The second half of this exercise is turning the head first to the right, and holding the position for thirty seconds, and then to the left, holding it for thirty seconds. When the head is turned the object is to attempt to bring the chin into alignment with the shoulder you are turning toward. (Figure 6.1)

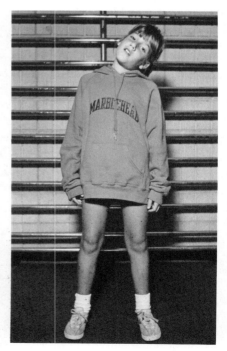

Figure 6.1.   Head circles.

BODY AREA: Shoulder
EXERCISE: Shoulder circles
PURPOSE: To stretch the shoulder, chest, and upper back muscles

Begin with the feet approximately shoulder-width apart, eyes forward, and arms held straight out to the side. Moving one arm at a time or both simultaneously, begin with small circular motions, gradually increasing the size of the circles. Movement should be performed both frontward and backward. This exercise should be done ten times in each direction for each shoulder. (Figure 6.2)

Figure 6.2   Shoulder circles.

BODY AREA: Waist
EXERCISE: Reaching side bends
PURPOSE: To stretch the muscles on the sides of the waist and back

Begin with both arms straight over the head, feet shoulder-width apart, and eyes forward. Slowly bend at the waist, first to one side, then to the other. The feeling of tightness will be felt at the waist and under the arm opposite to the side you are bending. This exercise should be held for ten seconds on each side and performed six times to each side. (Figure 6.3)

Figure 6.3   Reaching side bends.

BODY AREA: Back
EXERCISE: The seated Indian reach
PURPOSE: To stretch out the buttocks and lower back

Sit on the floor in an Indian position with legs folded and hands flat on the floor in front of you. Slowly slide both hands forward, bend at the waist, keep the back straight, and look directly ahead. Move forward until you feel slight tightness in the lower back and buttocks area. Hold this position for sixty seconds. Switch legs and do the exercise again. (Figure 6.4)

BODY AREA: Lower back
EXERCISE: Back press-downs
PURPOSE: To stretch the lower back (to correct lordosis, an excessive curvature in the lower spine)

Lie on your back with your eyes looking straight up, arms down by your side, legs straight, and ankles together. Tighten and push down with your stomach muscles, while tightening your buttocks muscles.

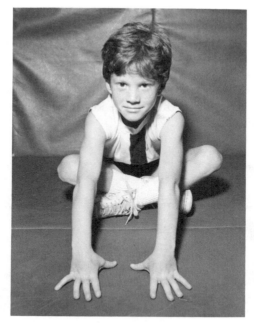

Figure 6.4   The seated Indian reach.

This action will flatten the lower back against the floor. Hold this position for a three count. Repeat this exercise for fifteen repetitions. (Figure 6.5)

Figure 6.5   Back press-downs.

BODY AREA: Chest
EXERCISE: Relaxed breathing
PURPOSE: To relax and practice controlled breathing

Lie on your back with your eyes looking straight up, arms up and next to the head, and legs straight. Slowly take a deep breath, hold it for a count of one, and gently exhale fully. Repeat this exercise ten to fifteen repetitions. (Figure 6.6)

Figure 6.6   Relaxed breathing.

BODY AREA: Front of thigh
EXERCISE: Lying quadriceps stretch
PURPOSE: To stretch the muscles of the front and outer sides of the thigh

Begin by lying on your side with the leg underneath you, pulled up so that the knee is bent and pointing directly in front of you, and the top leg is held with the knee straight. Support your head on the arm you are lying on. Bend the knee of the upper leg, and with the free hand grasp its ankle. The exercise is performed by slowly moving the heel toward the buttocks. When the heel can be moved three to four inches from the buttocks without pain in the front thigh, additional stretch can be produced by moving the foot toward the upper back while keeping the angle of the knee fixed. The knee of the leg you are lying on should still be pointing in front of you. Move until the feeling of slight tightness is felt in the front of the thigh. Relax and allow your knee to drop toward the floor. Hold this position for sixty seconds. Roll over and reverse legs. (Figure 6.7)

Figure 6.7   Lying quadriceps stretch.

BODY AREA: Front of hip
EXERCISE: The lunge
PURPOSE: To stretch the muscles of the front of the hip (hip flexors)

Begin with both feet together, hands on your hips or hanging down by your side for balance, and eyes forward. With the right foot take a big step forward. The front foot should be held flat. The back foot should have the heel off the ground and the knee should be straight. Keep the shoulders back, hips straight, and eyes forward. Bend your front knee as you move your pelvis forward and toward the ground. You should feel the stretch in the front of the hip and thigh of the back leg. In addition to stretching the hip of the back leg, this exercise will strengthen the quadriceps of the front leg.

It may be difficult initially to maintain this exercise for the entire sixty seconds. Begin slowly by maintaining the action point for ten, fifteen, or twenty seconds. You can use either the right or left leg to start with. If you can not hold the exercise for sixty seconds without resting, hold the position for as many seconds as you can, and then switch legs. After completing the same amount of time on the second leg, go back to the first leg and do another set. Continue to do the exercise until all of the sets add up to sixty seconds for each leg.

EXAMPLE: Peter can hold the lunge exercise position for fifteen seconds. He starts with the right leg (fifteen seconds), then switches to the left leg (fifteen seconds). Peter must do four sets of fifteen seconds to add up to sixty seconds.

As the young athlete continues to do the lunge exercise, the amount of time he or she can hold the position will increase. In Peter's case it went from fifteen seconds to twenty to thirty-five to forty-five to sixty. (Figure 6.8)

Figure 6.8   The lunge.

BODY AREA: Inner thigh (groin muscles)
EXERCISE: Wall split
PURPOSE: To stretch the groin muscles (upper inner thigh) and hamstrings (back of the thigh)

This exercise is best done using a wall, but can be done without one. Lie at the base of the wall, with your back on the floor, and your buttocks, legs, and heels on the wall. Keep your legs straight and slowly move your feet apart, sliding your heels along the wall until you feel a slight tightness in the inner portion of your thighs. Relax and hold this position for sixty seconds. For your parents' sake, this exercise should be performed without shoes. (Figure 6.9)

Figure 6.9   Wall split.

BODY AREA: Back of thigh
EXERCISE: Seated piked hamstring stretch
PURPOSE: To stretch the hamstring muscles

Sit on the floor with your legs straight out in front of you, toes pointing toward the ceiling, and ankles together. Place your hands on the
floor beside your knees. Look straight ahead and gently slide your hands
forward. Keep your back straight, your knees flat on the floor, and attempt to bring your chest as close to your knees and thighs as possible.
Stop when you feel slight tightness in the back of your thighs and knees.
Hold this position for sixty seconds. Remember, *no bouncing*. (Figure
6.10)

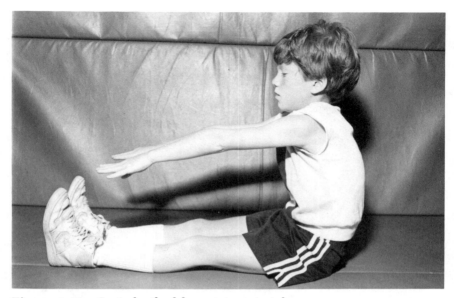

Figure 6.10   Seated piked hamstring stretch.

BODY AREA: Lower leg or calf
EXERCISE: Wall calf stretch
PURPOSE: To stretch the Achilles' tendon and the muscles of the calf

Stand with both feet approximately one to two feet from the wall. Take one foot and move it backward, keeping the toes pointed slightly inward. The heels of both feet must be kept flat on the floor during the exercise. Keep the head up, eyes forward, the back knee straight, the lower back flat, the shoulders and hips square. Bend the knee of the front leg and slowly move the pelvis forward toward the wall. *Do not lean forward.* Stop and make sure the back is flat. Hold the position when you feel a slight tightness in the upper part of the calf area (gastrocnemius). Do the exercise for both your right and left calves. Hold each leg for sixty seconds.

The second part of this exercise begins the same way, with both feet shoulder-width apart, approximately twelve to twenty-four inches from the wall. Slide one foot directly backward about twelve inches. Keeping both heels flat on the ground, bend both the front and back knees toward the feet until you feel slight tightness in the lower part of the calf area (soleus) of the back leg. Like the rest of the stretching exercises, hold the action point for sixty seconds. (Figure 6.11)

Figure 6.11   Wall calf stretch.

BODY AREA: Front of the lower leg (shin)
EXERCISE: Toe circles
PURPOSE: To stretch and warm the muscles of the front and sides
             of the lower leg

Sit with both legs straight out in front of you, toes pointing toward the ceiling, and ankles about twelve inches apart. Begin by pointing your toes away from you. Slowly move your feet in a circular motion. Make the largest circles you can, pointing your toes away, then out to the sides, then toward your knees, and finally toward each other. Perform this exercise fifteen times in both a clockwise and counterclockwise manner. (Figure 6.12)

EQUIPMENT CARE AND CONCERNS

The equipment supplying the resistance to the young athlete's muscles must be in top working condition. If machines such as a Universal or home gym are used, all of the working parts must be constantly checked and maintained. Special attention should be paid to the ends of the chains or wire cords that attach the weight stack on one end to the handles or bar on the other. The end of the cord that attaches to the

Figure 6.12   Toe circles.

machines will be located outside the home, the responsibility lies with someone else. The athlete, however, should always be aware of the equipment and its condition. Do not hesitate to bring a damaged piece of equipment to an employee's attention.

Free-weight care, on the other hand, requires slightly less attention to detail. Equipment such as benches and squat racks must be sturdy and able to support the weight of the barbell and/or the weight trainer safely. Equipment stability should not be a problem when dealing with the young athlete because of the relative lightness of both barbell and child. However, in the high school and college setting the equipment must be able to withstand greater weight. Equipment stability should be checked before any exercise is performed.

Free weights have a greater number of pieces than the machines. Strict attention should be placed on the tightness of the collars that are placed on the ends of the barbell or dumbbells to secure the plates. Sometimes handles, or hand grips, rides through a pulley or cam with every repetition. Occasionally, rubbing occurs due to a misalignment of the pulley, causing the cord to fray. If fraying occurs, immediate measures should be taken to correct the problem. The frayed cord should be replaced and the pulley straightened. Maintaining equipment is something that must become a part of the parent and child's daily/weekly routine. Since most the tightening screws in a collar become stripped. If stripping occurs, the collar should be replaced with one that can be tightened to prevent the plates from slipping.

Young athletes should be instructed in the proper care of the equipment. Through instruction they will better understand specific points of safety and can assist the adult (parent or gym instructor) in inspecting the equipment. With practice the participants learn the feel of the equipment, enabling them to identify an early problem before it becomes greater.

WEIGHT TRAINING SAFETY

While weight training, several rules should be followed to minimize potential hazards and possible tragedy.

1. Food and drinks, other than water in a plastic container, should not be present in the weight training area. It is best to drink water during a workout. Some sugar solutions may actually dehydrate the body by pulling water from the tissues into the intestine in order to dilute the high concentration of sugar. Glass bottles are a potential danger to everyone present in the area. Along with the danger of being cut by broken glass, the noise of a rolling bottle or breaking glass could disrupt the concentration of a child performing an exercise, which could cause the child to lose control of the weight and injure himself or herself or some-

Figure 6.13   Barbell and dumbell.

one else. This situation is more dangerous with free weights than with machines.

2. Eating in the weight room should be discouraged. The hormone insulin drives sugar (glucose) from the blood into the cells to be used as fuel. After one eats high-carbohydrate (sugary) foods, insulin is secreted into the bloodstream. These increased levels of insulin may cause drowsiness and fatigue. Crumbs on the floor are an invitation to bugs. Sticky hands that get on the barbell or plates are annoying to others using the equipment. There is no benefit in eating while you weight train. Eating should be left until after you have hit the showers.

3. Under no circumstances should anyone performing weight training exercises be allowed to chew gum. Gum may be pulled into the trachea (windpipe) when a deep breath is taken, and happens especially when the weight trainer lies flat on his or her back to perform an exercise such as the bench press. Gum pulled into the trachea can cause choking and possible serious injury. A dry mouth can easily be avoided by taking small sips of water.

4. When the young athlete is introduced to weight training, major emphasis must be placed on proper technique and safety. Improper execution of a weight training exercise invites injury and does not optimally work the muscles desired. Each exercise is performed to concentrate on a particular muscle or group of muscles. To use improper technique is to defeat the primary objective of the exercise. The careless athlete is not utilizing the workout to the best of his or her advantage. If an injury from improper technique occurs, the young athlete's development will be halted. When injury occurs, the athlete often has to stop or reduce participation for a period of time while healing takes place. The purpose of conditioning is to be physically ready for sports participation. Injuries of any kind are deterrents to success.

Research shows that improper technique is the primary cause of weight training injuries in both children and adults. As children grow through adolescence, boys in particular often suffer a shifting of focus from exercise technique to attempting to lift the greatest amount of weight they can "max out with." This showoff period is a potentially dangerous time and should be watched. The chance of injury becomes much greater when proper supervision, warm-up, or exercise technique is ignored.

SAFETY TIPS FOR THE WEIGHT TRAINER AT HOME

Following are some safety tips and general dos and don'ts that parents should observe in starting and maintaining a weight training program in their home.

DO . . . purchase name-brand equipment (weight set, bench, machine, belt, etc.) to ensure quality and safety. A junior high school or high school coach or a knowledgeable salesperson in a reputable sporting-goods store is a good resource for quality name brands.

DO . . . set up the equipment in an area that is clear of obstructions. An area in a basement, garage, or den is a good location for the weight training area.

DO . . . read the descriptions of each exercise found later in this chapter. It is important for the parent who is supervising the weight training program to know how to perform every exercise correctly.

DO . . . supervise and teach your child correct exercise technique.

DO . . . feel free to join in and weight train with your child. The flexibility and weight training exercises will benefit you both. Along with the physical benefits of better muscle tone will come the strengthening of emotional ties. When a parent becomes involved (not overinvolved), a special rapport usually develops.

DO . . . encourage and support your child through a weight training program. Your approval, pleasure, and enthusiasm can turn work into fun.

DO . . . make sure that collars are always used on barbells and dumbbells, and that they are tightened to prevent the plate from falling off.

DON'T . . . purchase a piece of equipment without making sure that it suits your child's purposes.

DON'T . . . set up the weight training area in a crowded room where the athlete may bump into things or someone may bump into the athlete. Cramped work areas are distracting and potentially dangerous.

DON'T . . . let a beginning weight trainer perform exercises without supervision.

DON'T . . . let a beginning weight trainer perform exercises without a spotter.

DON'T . . . use negative encouragement by asking, "Is that all you can do?" Whatever amount of weight or number of repetitions a child can correctly perform is great!

THE SPOTTER

An essential component in any safe weight training program is the spotter.

What is a spotter and what does a spotter do?

A spotter is a person who watches the weight trainer perform an exercise, provides assistance as needed, and supplies encouragement during the exercise. The spotter's purpose is to improve safety during the exercise in order to reduce the chance of injury and to monitor the weight trainer's exercise technique. The spotter must take the job seriously. Concentration on the exercise is as important for the spotter as for the athlete lifting the weight. A spotter does not stand around talking to others while his or her training partner is performing an exercise.

A spotter has several important responsibilities: (1) to make sure that the correct amount of weight is safely secured on each end of the barbell, or if dumbbells are used, that they are both the same weight; (2) to make sure that the weight trainer's body is positioned correctly to perform the exercise; (3) to watch and correct improper form while the weight trainer performs the exercise; (4) to provide appropriate verbal encouragement, such as, "Keep up the good work," "Push (or pull)," "That's it, keep going"; and (5) most importantly, to assist in lifting the weight if the weight trainer develops difficulty (give only enough assistance to provide smooth, continuous movement of the weight until completion of the exercise). (Note the spotter's responsibilities for each exercise presented at the end of this chapter.)

Who can be a spotter?

The only qualifications of a spotter are that he or she understands the proper technique of the exercise being performed (which will be detailed later in this chapter), and that he or she is strong enough to assist the weight trainer with the weight being used. These qualifications include parents, friends, coaches, brothers or sisters, or other relatives. A spotter can be anyone who will be encouraging and helpful. Weight training with a partner allows both individuals to learn and perfect their weight training technique while sharing some common healthy experiences. Verbal encouragement is usually added incentive to stick to the weight program and to continue giving your best.

When assisting the lifter in completing the last repetition, there are several methods that can be used. Figures 6.14 and 6.16 demonstrate the two best methods for spotting weight training exercises. The method you choose is totally dependent upon the weight trainer's preference, the strength of the spotter, and the ability of the spotter to position himself or herself well for the exercise. Some exercises are more difficult for the spotter, who must position himself or herself around the equipment.

Figure 6.14 demonstrates the first method, with the spotter supporting the bar from underneath. This method is probably the most widely used. It is essential that the spotter supply even pressure on the bar with both hands. Figure 6.15 demonstrates what can happen if unequal pressure is supplied to the bar by the spotter.

The second spotting method, as shown in figure 6.16, provides con-

Figure 6.14   Spotter's assistance (first method).

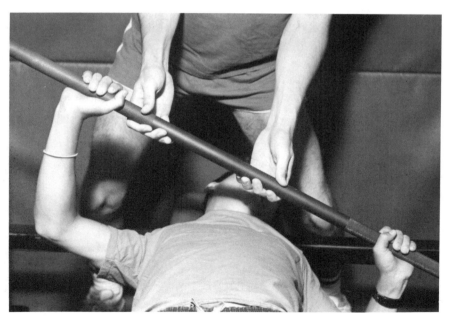

Figure 6.15   Spotter's incorrect assistance (first method).

tinuous movement of the weight by pushing or pulling on the weight trainer's body. Notice that the athlete performing the behind-the-head shoulder press has a spotter pushing on his elbows.

Figure 6.17 demonstrates the proper technique for spotting a person throughout the entire execution of the exercise. It is highly recommended that the parent instruct each child on how to be a good spotter as well as a safe weight trainer. By teaching children how to weight train and spot one another correctly, you will establish a safe, enjoyable, healthy, and effective experience.

WEIGHT TRAINING PSYCHOLOGY

Competition is an excellent motivator for most people in a weight training environment. However, emphasis should be placed on performing an exercise correctly and competing against oneself rather than against other athletes.

The first priority parents and weight room instructors have when setting up a weight training program is developing an atmosphere of self-competition. This feeling of competing against oneself in the weight room depends heavily on what the parent does and says. Positive comments made at home can contribute to a young athlete's motivation. Expressing pride in a child for performing three workouts the past week,

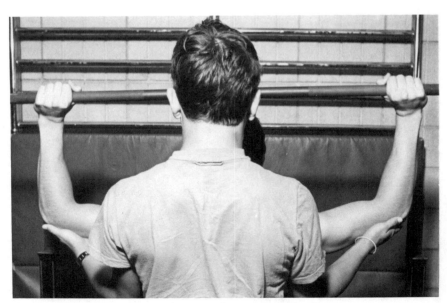

Figure 6.16   Spotter's assistance (second method).

for adding another repetition, for increasing the amount of weight of an exercise, or for the recognizable change you can see in his or her body can have a tremendously positive effect. Do not hesitate to encourage your child.

DEVELOPING A WEIGHT TRAINING PROGRAM

When setting up a weight training program, there are several points that must be considered: the age of the child; the size of the child; the child's weight training experience; the number of exercises; the num-

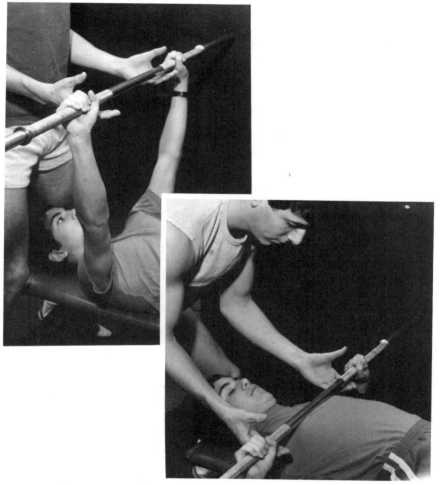

Figure 6.17   Execution of an exercise with spotter.

ber of sets of each exercise; the number of repetitions per set; and the duration, frequency, and intensity of the program.

When should my child begin to weight train?

This excellent question may be answered several ways. Before the age of seven, eight, or nine, a child may or may not have the attention span or the neuromuscular coordination to perform exercises the correct way consistently. Before eight years or age, most children focus their attention on play, not competition. For this age group muscular development, like skill development, is best achieved by practicing and participating in the sport or sports.

When a child reaches nine or ten years of age, many sports become team- and league-oriented. This change to competitive status places new physical and emotional stresses on the child. At this point a child may be ready to begin a conditioning type of program. However, it is important that only light resistance be used in the program, and the exercises be fun and gamelike. Weight training exercises should be performed with a book or other light object for resistance. Small one- to two-pound dumbbells can be purchased if desired. A free-weight set including barbell, dumbbell, and plates is not necessary at this time.

When can my child start using free weights?

When the child has demonstrated proper exercise technique with lighter resistance items such as a book, free weights can be introduced. If the child wishes, after one set of fifteen repetitions can easily be performed with a light dumbbell, he or she can begin using free weights. Use the dumbbells first. They can be purchased in increments of one, two, two and one-half, three, and five pounds. However, be aware that dumbbells are more difficult to balance and stabilize than a single bar of equal weight.

If your child is eleven or twelve years old and wishes to start a weight training program, it is best to begin with one- or two-pound dumbbells, which allow the body to learn the proper exercise techniques with a comfortable weight (resistance). After mastering perfect exercise technique, a child can move up to using the empty barbell (without any added plates) or adjustable dumbbells. Most empty dumbbells weigh five pounds and the empty barbell usually weighs twenty pounds. A *small* progression of increasing weight (resistance) must *always* be used with the young weight trainer. When the weight trainer is able to perform the maximum number of repetitions per set, every set of that exercise, for four workouts in a row, one and one-half or two and one-half pounds of resistance may be added to the dumbbell or barbell respectively.

At twelve and thirteen years of age, or older, a child who wishes to start weight training should begin with three- to five-pound dumbbells, or the empty dumbbell bars of a free-weight set. After the child masters the exercise techniques, use of the empty barbell should be included for the appropriate exercises. Additional weight can be added to a dumbbell or barbell in the smallest increment available, usually two and one-half pounds (two plates, one and one-quarter pounds each) or five pounds (two plates, two and one-half pounds each).

Increased resistance should be added only when the athlete correctly performs the maximum number of repetitions in every set, for three consecutive workouts. Each time the child increases the weight of an exercise, special attention should be paid to proper technique. If the child struggles with the new weight and can not perform the minimum number of repetitions, he or she should drop back to the lighter weight. *Struggling* in this context means squirming around, preventing proper technique from being performed.

Adolescents fourteen years old and older should be able to start weight training with the empty barbell and dumbbells. They should be able to add weight whenever they are able to perform the maximum number of repetitions for every set of the exercise, two or three workouts in a row. As an athlete gets older, the number of sets and repetitions per exercise may vary. For example, a fifteen- or sixteen-year-old with a year or two of weight training experience will be able to increase the weight, decrease the number of repetitions, and increase the number of sets of specific exercises. This increase in exercise intensity will enhance the strength development of older athletes.

How long should a training session last?

The word *duration* in a weight training program refers to the amount of time between sets and the time needed for each workout session. For the beginner, each training session should last no longer than an hour and one-half (ninety minutes). If the young athlete moves from set to set and exercise to exercise, the entire weight training program should last no longer than one hour. This is dependent upon the number of exercises and sets per exercise performed. A warm-up including pre-stretching and stretching exercises should take approximately fifteen to twenty minutes. The cool-down involving some stretching and brisk walking should last approximately ten minutes.

Young people can learn concentration and discipline while weight training. If athletes have unlimited time in the weight room, they become more easily distracted and lose their concentration, which can be dangerous. Weight training can easily become a socially oriented activity. There is nothing wrong with this as long as the athlete does not waste time. It is best to discourage excessive talking while weight training. After becoming distracted, the athlete may not feel like finishing the workout.

The question of time between sets is a common one, with several good answers. The real answer is that it depends upon the results you want. If the athlete is looking to develop muscular strength and size, he or she needs an appropriate time between sets to allow the muscles to recover completely. For strength development a rest of between one to two minutes is recommended. If an athlete does not feel recovered in that period of time, however, the rest period should be extended.

A wrestler, who requires both endurance and strength in his muscles, needs a shorter period of forty-five to ninety seconds between sets. A cross-country runner who wants to improve his or her strength and power, yet does not want to interfere with endurance, should rest thirty to fifty seconds between sets. As the rest period between sets becomes shorter, the weights used should become lighter.

The times given for the rest periods are only recommended. Each child is different. When a child is just beginning to weight train, longer rest periods are recommended. The athlete should not feel rushed between sets. Remember, this is *fun*.

How intense should the workout be?

Intensity is the degree of effort needed to perform an exercise. Younger athletes will perform their exercises with a small amount of intensity, whereas the older athletes will use more. Intensity is one of the major aspects of a weight training program. By altering the intensity of a workout, you can use the same exercises for virtually every sport. A muscle develops strength, endurance, and size by adapting to the greater demands placed upon it through daily activities, or artificial means such as weight training. The greater the demand placed on the muscle, the greater adaptation occurs. Caution must be used when deciding on the intensity of a weight training program. Too much will prohibit strength development.

For the beginner the intensity of weight training is not an issue. The beginner should concentrate solely on technique and form, using light weights and a moderate number of repetitions (table 6.1). The intermediate weight trainer who has consistently shown the responsibility of using proper technique and a strong desire to learn, can be instructed on how to increase the intensity of the workout.

To increase the intensity of an exercise, a heavier weight is used to perform the exercise. When a heavier weight is used, fewer repetitions can be performed. Initially, however, one *forced* repetition at the end of the last two sets is a good way to begin increasing an exercise's intensity. A forced repetition is the last repetition of the set, in which the weight trainer needs the assistance of the spotter to complete the exercise. As the adolescent matures and becomes older, eccentric or negative work may be added to the lifting program. The high school athlete who wishes to gain weight and become stronger for a particular sport or for a personal goal, must learn how to increase the intensity of his or her workouts.

Table 6.1 shows the maximum amount of intensity that should be used by athletes of a particular age. These are maximum numbers. For the athlete who does not wish to increase his or her muscle size, yet still develop some strength, lighter weights should be used with higher repetitions and two to three sets of each exercise should be performed.

Table 6.1. Maximum workout intensity.

	Regimen by Age Group			
	10–12	12–14	14–16	17 +
Exercises per body part	1	1	2	>2
Sets	1-2	2-3	3-4	4-6
Repetitions	12-15	10-12	8-10	6-10
Weight	very light	light	moderate	heavy
Forced repetitions	no	no	yes	yes

With what frequency should the exercises be performed?

The *frequency* of workouts and time between workouts (recovery) are important components of every weight training program, particularly for the beginner. A muscle needs to be exercised, but also requires time to recover and grow. Recovery involves sleep time and the adequate rest given to the particular muscles exercised. Sleep is necessary for optimal recovery of the muscle. A muscle does not grow while it is being exercised. It grows during the period of rest.

A muscle should not be rigorously exercised more than every other day and no less than three times a week for best development. If the weight training program involves exercising muscles of the entire body on the same day, which a beginner and intermediate will use, a three-day schedule such as Monday–Wednesday–Friday, Sunday–Tuesday–Thursday, or Tuesday–Thursday–Saturday is appropriate. It is important to be consistent with the workouts and not work the same muscle groups two consecutive days.

RECORDKEEPING

When beginning a weight training program, a child can be very susceptible to feelings of inadequacy. Keeping a written record of a growing athlete's progress is the best motivator. It is important that the child actively take part in this recording process.

A simple, inexpensive notebook can be used for recordkeeping. Table 6.2 shows one method of organizing records. Each exercise has its own page. On each page is left a space for the date, weight used, and number of repetitions (reps) per set.

Table 6.3 shows the method whereby each workout is listed together on a page. In this case space is left for the exercise in addition to the date, weight used, and number of reps per set.

Table 6.2   Record of bench-press exercises.

BENCH PRESS

Date	Weight/Reps		
	Set 1	Set 2	Set 3
5/9/87	55/15	55/14	55/13
5/11/87	55/15	55/15	55/14
5/13/87	55/15	55/15	55/15

Table 6.3   General workout record.

May 9, 1987   Saturday

Exercise	Weight/Reps		
	Set 1	Set 2	Set 3
Squat	100/15	100/13	100/13
Bench press	55/15	55/15	55/14
Behind-head press	45/15	45/14	45/13
Partial curl	20	18	18

EXERCISE TECHNIQUE

When performing an exercise, the weight trainer should heed basic rules of procedure:

ALWAYS use correct technique to work the desired muscles optimally and to reduce the chance of injury.

ALWAYS perform an exercise through a complete range of motion.

ALWAYS have the weight under total control.

ALWAYS consider safety first. Make sure there is a spotter present when performing the exercises that require one.

ALWAYS breath in a smooth, controlled fashion. *Do not hold your breath.*

Why should an exercise be performed through a full range of motion?

All exercises should be performed through a full range of motion to ensure that the muscle develops the greatest amount of strength. In addition, the joint that the muscle acts on develops the greatest range of motion, thereby allowing greater use of the new strength.

How fast should an exercise be performed?

When performing an exercise, the weight trainer should *always* have control of the weight, especially when using free weights. Having control of the weight means that the athlete lowers and raises the weight at a constant speed without swaying side to side or fighting to maintain his or her balance. The Nautilus system recommends the 2-4 method of muscle contraction (concentric contraction, 2 seconds, and eccentric contraction, 4 seconds). In other words, pushing or pulling the weight should take two seconds and returning the weight back to the starting position should take four seconds. This method adequately involves both concentric and eccentric muscle contraction. By training only concentrically, you ignore one-half of optimal muscle conditioning.

The 2-4 method can also be used with any other type of weight training equipment. The beginning weight trainer should count the seconds out loud as he or she performs the exercises. Counting will develop the timing necessary to control the weight. This control develops greater strength and a safe training technique. Counting out loud will also prevent the weight trainer from holding his or her breath.

When should the weight trainer increase the weight of an exercise?

The general rule of thumb for athletes thirteen years old and older is that when they can perform all of their sets of an exercise using the maximum number of repetitions, three workouts in a row, it is time to add weight. For example, if thirteen-year-old Jared performs three sets of twelve repetitions of the biceps curl on Monday, Wednesday, and again on Friday, the weight used to perform the exercise can be increased two and one-half to five pounds at the following workout on Monday. Athletes twelve years old and younger should perform four workouts of maximum repetitions for every set of an exercise before additional weight is used. For example, if twelve-year-old Beth can perform three sets of twelve repetitions of the triceps extension on Monday, she should attempt to repeat this performance on Wednesday, Friday, and the following Monday. If successful, she can increase the weight by two and one-half pounds on the following Wednesday. Table 6.1 lists the range of repetitions by age group of weight trainers that should be used for an exercise.

How much weight should be added when the weight trainer is ready to increase the weight of an exercise?

The increase in weight on a dumbbell is going to be smaller than that on a barbell. For athletes who are thirteen years old and younger, the smallest increment should be used on both the dumbbells and barbells, usually two and one-half pounds (two plates, one and one-quarter pounds each). For the athletes who are fourteen years old and older, the increase can be two and one-half pounds on a dumbbell and five pounds (two plates, two and one-half pounds each) on a barbell. As the athlete becomes an accomplished weight trainer, increases of five and ten pounds on a dumbbell and barbell respectively are not uncommon. Regardless of age, however, if the athlete can not perform the minimum number of repetitions recommended, the increased weight should be lowered.

EXERCISE NOTES

Before reviewing the following free-weight exercises, you should note the seven components of each and what information each provides. If your child will be starting on a machine, the information pertaining to the muscles being used, exercise technique (starting position and exercise performance), and breathing will still apply.

Equipment. The equipment needed to perform these exercises correctly is minimal. Companies manufacturing exercise equipment are constantly upgrading and developing new apparatus. Complicated and expensive equipment, however, is not needed for successful weight training. For the following exercises you will need a straight barbell bar with two collars; two dumbbell bars, each with two collars; paired plates (weight) for each side of the bar, in various weight increments (the most common include one and one-quarter, two and one-half, five, ten, and twenty-five pounds); a bench press (weight lifting) bench (figure 6. 18) that is sturdy and includes at least two extended poles on one end that support the barbell; and a weight lifting belt (for athletes large enough for it to fit properly). A home multi-exercise machine, while practical for the performance of these exercises, is optional.

Target Muscles. The weight trainer should concentrate on the specific muscles being exercised. This concentration facilitates proper exercise technique. Figure 6.19 identifies the muscles and their location.

Starting Position. Note the proper position of the weight trainer's body in relation to the barbell or dumbbell before starting the exercise. A barbell or dumbbell is held with either an overhand or underhand grip. An overhand grip (figure 6.20) is used when the weight trainer places his or her hands on top of the bar such that the back of the hands can be easily seen and the palms are facing away. An underhand grip (figure 6.21) is used when the weight trainer grips the bar from underneath, with palms away from the body.

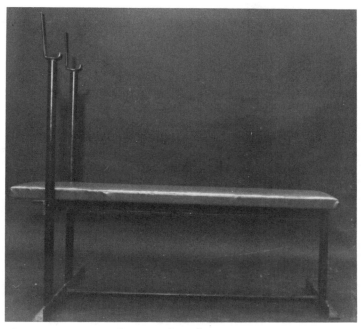

Figure 6.18   Bench-press bench.

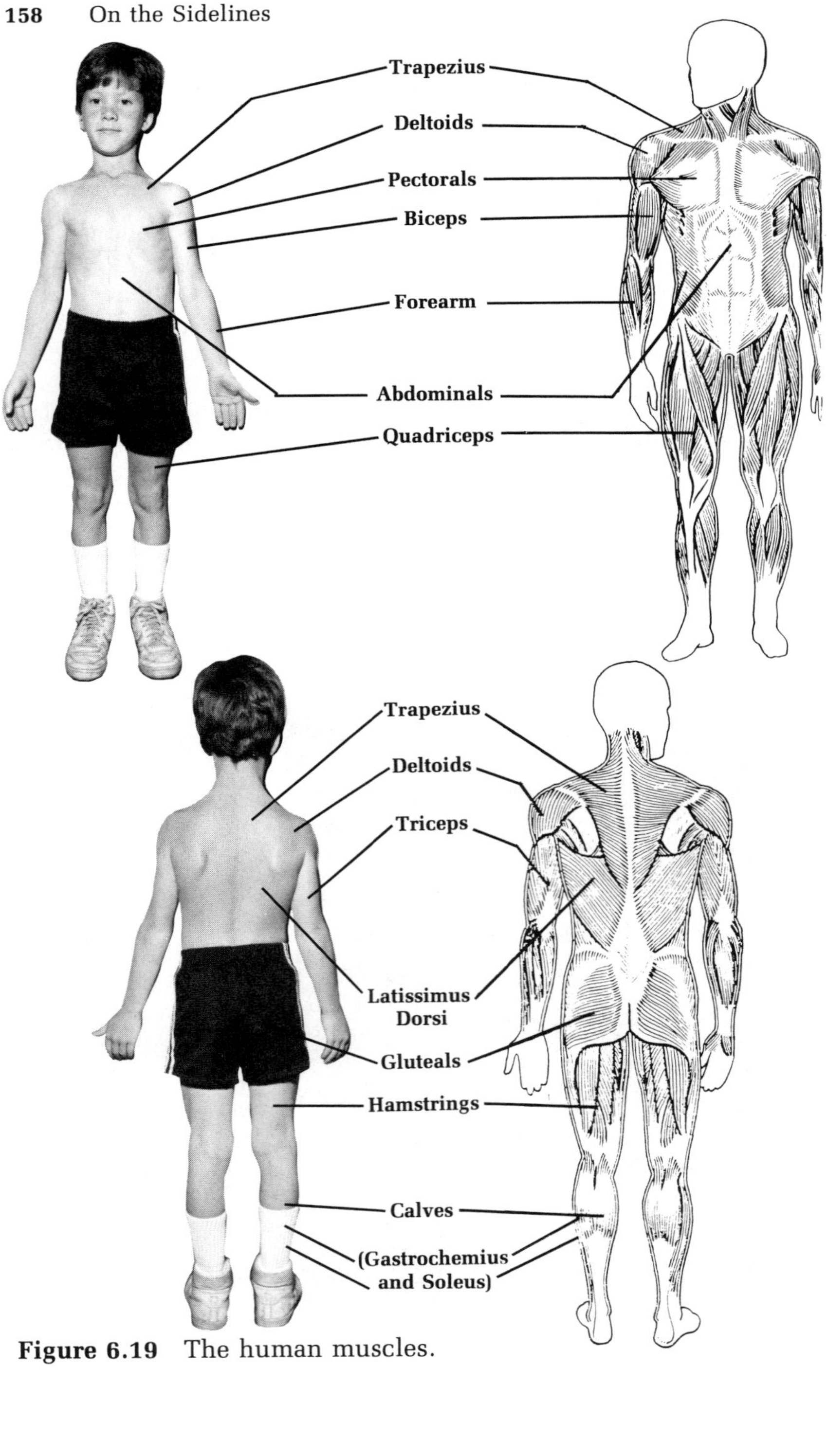

Figure 6.19   The human muscles.

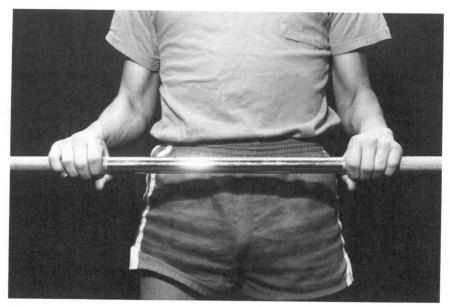

Figure 6.20   Overhand grip.

Figure 6.21   Underhand grip.

Exercise Performance. The proper way to do the exercise is described, including the locations of specific parts of the body from the starting position through the exercise movement and back to the starting position for the next repetition.

Special Considerations. Specific techniques or safety factors that are unique to the exercise are included.

Breathing. The proper breathing rhythm for performing the specific exercise is described.

Spotter's Responsibilities. The body position and responsibilities of the spotter, if needed, are described.

Each exercise includes several photographs, which show the correct starting and finishing positions. The pictures are intended to reinforce the written descriptions. This combination of words and pictures will enable the parent and child with little or no weight training experience to perform each exercise correctly and confidently.

BASIC WEIGHT TRAINING PROGRAM FOR CHILDREN

EXERCISE: One-quarter squat

EQUIPMENT: Two dumbbells (beginners) and a barbell and support rack (intermediate and advanced)

TARGET MUSCLES: Quadriceps, hamstrings, buttocks, and lower back

STARTING POSITION: Dumbbells: Grip both dumbbells such that the palms of each hand face each other and your arms are hanging down by your sides. Barbell: The bar should rest across the top of the shoulders with both hands in the overhand grip, positioned on the bar slightly wider than shoulder-width apart. The head should be kept up, with the eyes forward or looking at the top of the wall in front of you. This position helps keep the weight trainer's back straight. Feet should be approximately shoulder-width apart and the toes pointed slightly outward. To make balancing easier, two weight plates about an inch in thickness or a two-by-four piece of wood approximately thirty-six inches long can be used to elevate the athlete's heels. Elevated heels make the exercise easier for athletes with tight Achilles' tendons.

EXERCISE PERFORMANCE: Bend both knees and slowly lower the buttocks and hips, keeping the back straight and the head up. Keep both feet flat on the floor throughout the exercise. As you get closer to the floor, your upper body will move slightly forward and your buttocks will move slightly backward to maintain balance. Lower the body until the thighs are halfway between the starting position and parallel with

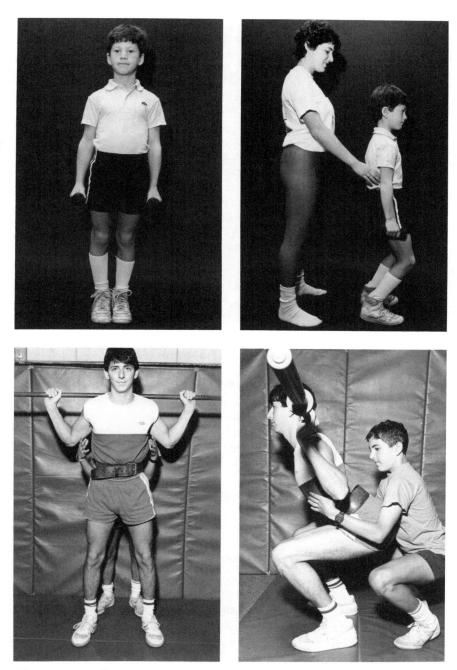

Figure 6.22   One-quarter squat.

the floor. Stop for a second. Push upward with a slightly faster yet controlled motion. While pushing upward concentrate on using the thigh muscles to do the work.

SPECIAL CONSIDERATIONS: This is a very difficult exercise and should only be performed when proper supervision is available. The athlete and the spotter should go through the exercise without a weight to familiarize themselves with the exercise. If using dumbbells, make sure the shoulders are level and the athlete is not leaning on one side, and if a barbell is used, look to see that the weight remains equally distributed across the shoulders. The back should be straight and the eyes focused on the top of the wall in front of you. A towel or other form of padding should be wrapped around the middle portion of a barbell or placed across the top of the shoulders in order to reduce the pressure on the base of the neck and to make things more comfortable. A weight training belt should be worn, if the athlete is big enough, to help support the lower back.

BREATHING: Take a deep breath as you lower your hips. Slowly exhale as you push the weight up to the starting position.

SPOTTER'S RESPONSIBILITIES: Spotting is absolutely necessary in the squat. A single spotter can stand behind with arms under but not touching those of the weight trainer. If the athlete has difficulty with balance or completing the exercise, the spotter smoothly pulls upward, keeping the athlete's back straight. The spotter can take the dumbbells from the athlete's hands if he or she gets too tired. If the exercise is performed with a barbell, the spotter can guide the weight back to the supports or take the weight from the shoulders of the athlete. Remember, a spotter must *always* pay attention when the athlete is performing the exercise.

EXERCISE: One-armed dumbbell rowing

EQUIPMENT NEEDED: One dumbbell and a bench approximately knee height

TARGET MUSCLES: Latissimus dorsi (lats), rear deltoid, and teres major

STARTING POSITION: Place the left knee on the end of the bench and the right foot flat on the floor to the right of the bench keeping the knee straight. Bend at the waist, placing the left hand on the bench and keeping the elbow straight. Grasp the dumbbell in the right hand with the palm facing toward the bench. The right arm should hang straight away from the body. Lift your head such that you are looking directly in front of you. This position will help keep the back straight and flat. To per-

Figure 6.23   One-armed dumbbell rowing.

form the exercise with the left arm, switch body positions by substituting right for left and left for right in the above description.

EXERCISE PERFORMANCE: Keeping the back straight and flat, bend the right elbow and smoothly pull the dumbbell up to the body until it touches the right shoulder and chest. Hold this position for a count of one, and smoothly lower the dumbbell to the starting position. The right upper arm should be kept close to the body during the pulling and lowering motion. The elbow of the moving arm should point toward the ceiling when the dumbbell is touching the shoulder.

SPECIAL CONSIDERATIONS: Be sure to keep the back flat and the head up. While doing this exercise, do not swing or jerk the dumbbell. This action will place stress on the athlete's back, increasing the chance of injury.

BREATHING: Take a moderately deep breath, then begin to pull the dumbbell up toward the chest, smoothly exhaling, until the dumbbell reaches the body. Smoothly inhale as the weight is lowered to the starting position.

SPOTTER'S RESPONSIBILITIES: Watch the weight trainer's back to make sure it remains straight and level throughout the set. See that the dumbbell is brought up high enough to touch the chest, while keeping the arm close to the body.

EXERCISE: Standing biceps curl

EQUIPMENT NEEDED: A barbell or two dumbbells

TARGET MUSCLES: Biceps and forearm

STARTING POSITION: Stand with feet approximately shoulder-width apart. Bend the knees and grasp the barbell that is on the floor in front of you, with the underhand grip (palms facing away from you) about shoulder-width apart. Using the legs, keep the back straight, head up, and stand up straight such that the barbell rests across the thighs. Look straight ahead and keep your knees slightly bent. Your elbows should be snug to the sides of your rib cage.

EXERCISE PERFORMANCE: Keep your back straight, your knees slightly bent, and your elbows snug to your sides. Bend your elbows and bring the barbell up such that your hands (and the bar) come close to your shoulders. Hold the position for a count of one, and smoothly lower the barbell back to the starting position.

SPECIAL CONSIDERATIONS: A weight lifting belt can be used to ensure that the athlete minimizes using the back muscles to assist the movement. The knees should be kept slightly bent to protect the lower back from added stress.

BREATHING: Smoothly exhale as you raise the dumbbell/barbell up toward the shoulders. Slowly inhale as you lower the weight to the starting position.

SPOTTER'S RESPONSIBILITIES: A spotter is not necessary unless the athlete can not complete a repetition. In this case the spotter should stand in front of the athlete and assist by gently pushing up on the weight.

EXERCISE: Bench press

EQUIPMENT NEEDED: A sturdy bench-press bench with two supports to hold a barbell, or a sturdy, narrow bench approximately thirty-six inches in length to use with dumbbells

TARGET MUSCLES: Pectoralis major, deltoid, and triceps

STARTING POSITION: With your back flat on the bench, lie such that the barbell that is resting safely in the supports is directly over your nose.

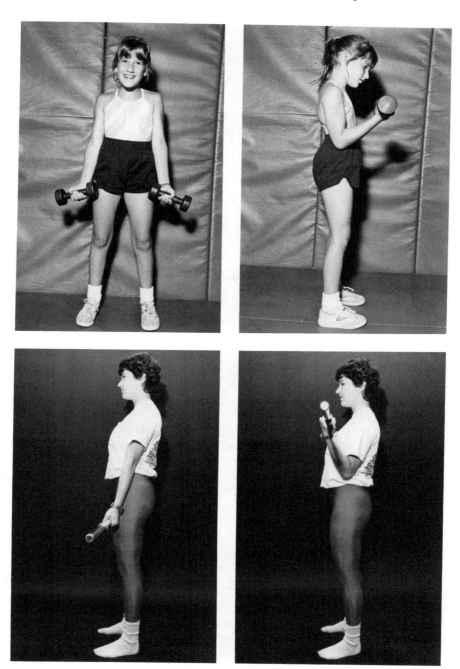

Figure 6.24   Standing biceps curl.

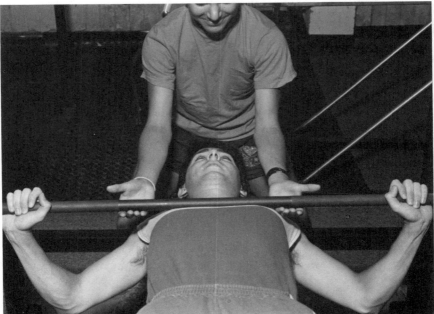

Figure 6.25   Bench press.

Using an overhand grip, place your hands approximately shoulder-width apart on the barbell. Lift the weight off the supports and balance the barbell over your chest with the arms straight.

EXERCISE PERFORMANCE: Smoothly lower the barbell until it lightly touches the chest at nipple level. As the barbell is lowered, the elbows should move out to the side, lining up directly under the hands. When the elbows are in the proper position, the forearms are perpendicular to the floor when the bar is approximately halfway through the exercise. When the barbell touches the chest, stop for a count of one, then smoothly push the bar up to the starting position.

SPECIAL CONSIDERATIONS: To increase stability and decrease stress on the lower back, both feet should be placed comfortably on the floor. If the bench is too high and the feet do not touch the floor, the feet can be supported by blocks of wood or a stack of books. With the feet on the floor or supports, the knees should be at the level of the bench or above, not below. By having the knees bent and above the level of the bench, the lower back should be flat on the bench and not arched. Also, the elbows should always be directly under the bar. When viewed from the side, the elbows, arms, and barbell (or dumbbell) should be in vertical alignment.

BREATHING: Take a deep breath and lift the barbell off the top of the supports. Exhale as you are balancing the weight with straight arms. Take a deep breath as you are slowly lowering the bar. As you begin to push the bar up, smoothly exhale as if you are blowing the bar up to the top (arms straight). Never hold your breath!

SPOTTER'S RESPONSIBILITIES: Stand at the weight trainer's head near the barbell supports. Using either of the spotting techniques discussed earlier in the chapter, always have your hands about two inches from either the barbell or the weight trainer's elbows. See that the weight (either barbell or dumbbell) does not sway too much and remains level throughout the exercise. Make sure that the weight trainer does not arch his or her back while performing the exercise. Excessive arching of the back may lead to lower back injury. You should not be able to slide your hand under the athlete's lower back at any time (before or during the performance of the exercise).

EXERCISE: Seated behind-the-head press

EQUIPMENT NEEDED: A weight training bench or very steady chair with a high back, two dumbbells or a barbell

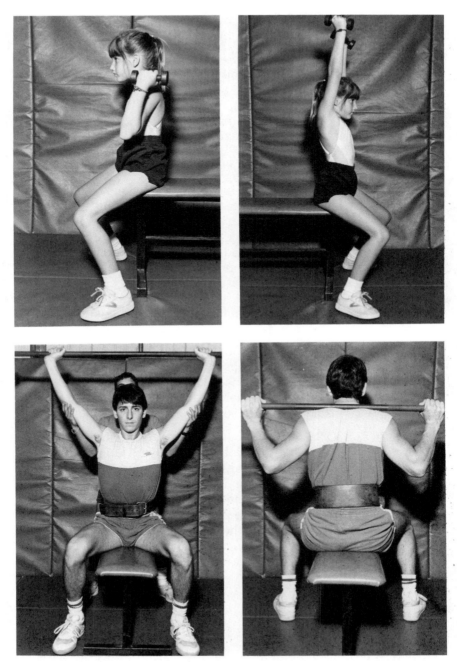

Figure 6.26   Seated behind-the-head press.

TARGET MUSCLES: Deltoids, trapezius, and triceps

STARTING POSITION: Sit with your back against the back of the chair or on the bench, with both feet flat on the floor. Dumbbells should be held at shoulder height with the palms facing each other, and the elbows held to the side and under the weight. The barbell should lie across the top of the shoulders behind the head with the hands held approximately shoulder-width apart and palms facing forward toward the direction you are looking. The elbows should be held out to the side, directly under the hands and/or barbell.

EXERCISE PERFORMANCE: Smoothly push the weight directly upward, fully straightening the arms. Keep the elbows, hands, and bar in vertical alignment. This action is to ensure the best leverage and power. Hold the weight over the head for a count of one, and slowly lower the weight to the starting position.

SPECIAL CONSIDERATIONS: Be careful that you *do not arch your back* while performing the exercise. In the beginning the weight will wobble and sway when it is over the weight trainer's head. The spotter should pay special attention to this problem, particularly for the first two weeks. After several workouts the muscles that stabilize the movement will become strong enough to control the weight.

BREATHING: Take a deep breath while the weight is at shoulder level and smoothly exhale while pushing the barbell or dumbbell up to the straight-arm position. Breathe in as the weight is lowered and returned to shoulder level.

SPOTTER'S RESPONSIBILITIES: You may have to help bring the weight up to the athlete's shoulders. During the exercise, stand behind the weight trainer such that you can be in the best position to spot the weight or the weight trainer's elbows. Standing behind allows you to be closest to the weight if you are needed and to make sure that the weight trainer does not arch his or her back during the performance of the exercise.

EXERCISE: Lying triceps extension

EQUIPMENT NEEDED: A barbell or two dumbells

TARGET MUSCLES: Triceps, chest, back, and forearm

STARTING POSITION: Lie on your back on the floor with your feet flat and your knees pointing toward the ceiling. Grip the two dumbbells, which are balanced on one end next to your head, with the palms facing each other. Lift the dumbbells off the floor such that your elbows are

Figure 6.27   Lying triceps extension.

pointing toward the ceiling and the weights are resting next to your ears. For a barbell, lie in the same position with the bar positioned on the ground over your head. Grip it using an overhand grip such that the palms of the hands face toward the ceiling with hands six to eight inches apart. Pull the barbell off the floor such that your elbows are pointing directly up toward the ceiling. The barbell should begin at the level of the forehead or slightly above the top of the head.

EXERCISE PERFORMANCE: Keep the elbows pointing up toward the ceiling while you smoothly straighten your arms all the way. Hold this position for a count of one, and smoothly lower the barbell to the starting position.

SPECIAL CONSIDERATIONS: A barbell should be used by athletes who can easily handle fifteen-pound dumbbells and not before. The action should always be smooth and under control. Wobbling and instability will probably occur when the arms are fully straightened. This action will occur for several workouts until the stabilizing muscles can be adequately strengthened. When using a barbell, weights should always be secured by collars.

BREATHING: Smoothly exhale as you straighten your arms. Slowly inhale as the barbell is lowered to the starting position.

SPOTTER'S RESPONSIBILITIES: The spotter should kneel at the athlete's head and keep his or her hands in the ready position to grasp the barbell.

EXERCISE: Heel raise

EQUIPMENT NEEDED: A barbell and support rack or two dumbbells, and a two-by-four three feet long

TARGET MUSCLES: Gastrocnemius and soleus (calf)

STARTING POSITION: As in the squat, the two dumbbells should be held in each hand or the barbell should be placed across the top of the shoulders behind the head. Using the overhand-palms-forward grip on the barbell, grasp the bar comfortably wider than shoulder width. The balls of the feet are placed on a two-by-four piece of wood with the heels touching the floor. The feet should be approximately twelve inches apart and the toes are pointed straight ahead. The head is up with eyes forward, and the back and knees are straight.

EXERCISE PERFORMANCE: Maintain starting body position and simply rise up on the toes, getting the heels as high off the floor as possi-

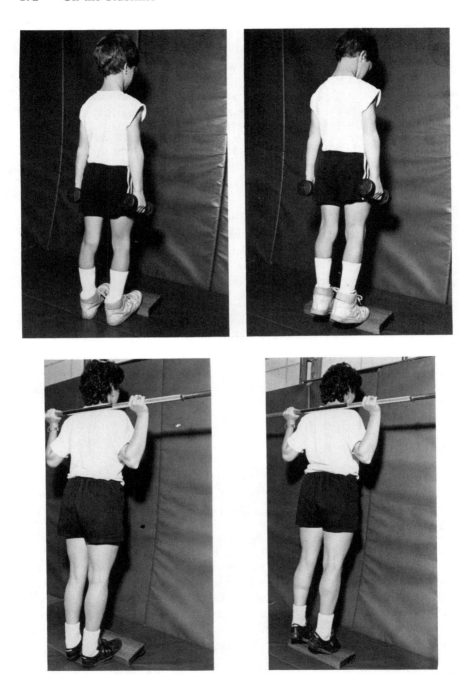

Figure 6.28   Heel raise.

ble. Hold the up position for a count of one, and slowly lower your heels back to the starting position.

SPECIAL CONSIDERATIONS: Begin without using any weight to get used to the feeling of balancing on your toes on top of the two-by-four. Keep the back and knees straight and the head up.

BREATHING: Smoothly exhale as you go up on your toes and inhale as you return to the starting position.

SPOTTER'S RESPONSIBILITIES: The spotter should stand behind the weight trainer with hands under the athlete's arms. The major problem to watch for is the weight trainer's balance.

EXERCISE: Partial curl or crunch

EQUIPMENT: A soft yet firm floor and a bench or chair

TARGET MUSCLES: Abdominals (stomach)

STARTING POSITION: Lie on your back with your lower legs resting on top of the bench or chair, or if a partner is available, he or she can hold them. Your lower legs should be parallel and your thighs perpendicular to the floor. As in all sit-up-type exercises, the chin should be tucked to the chest and the back of the head and neck off the floor. Hands and arms can be held alongside the body (easiest), across the chest (difficult), or behind the head (most difficult).

EXERCISE PERFORMANCE: Using your stomach muscles, lift your hips slightly off the floor, bring your shoulders and back off the floor, and touch your elbows and eventually shoulders to your knees. Hold this position for a count of one, then slowly lower your lower back then middle back and finally your shoulders to the floor.

SPECIAL CONSIDERATIONS: A variation in this exercise can be done by twisting the waist and touching the right elbow or shoulder to the left knee and then the left elbow or shoulder to the right knee. This exercise is more difficult than the regular sit-up and should be attempted only after the athlete can do ten regular sit-ups in a row. If a single partial curl can not be done, negative partial curls can be attempted. This exercise requires the assistance of a spotter to hold the athlete in the up position with his or her elbows touching the knees. The spotter lets the athlete go such that he or she can slowly lower himself or herself back to the floor. After several workouts of three to eight negative partial curls, the athlete will be ready to perform one or more repetitions of a regular partial curl.

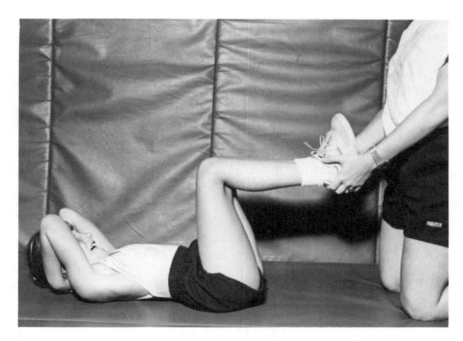

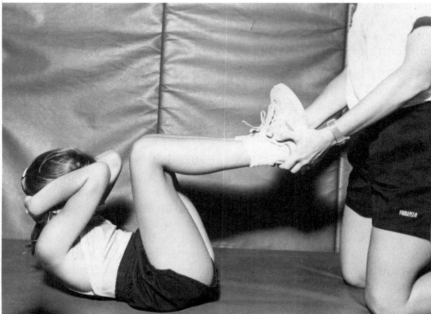

Figure 6.29   Partial curl or crunch.

BREATHING: Smoothly exhale as you pull yourself up to touch your knees, and hold for a count of one. Inhale as you lower yourself to the starting position.

SPOTTER'S RESPONSIBILITIES: A spotter is not necessary unless negative repetitions are performed.

EXERCISE: Advanced bicycle

EQUIPMENT NEEDED: A soft yet firm surface (such as a rug or towel on the floor)

TARGET MUSCLES: Abdominals (stomach)

STARTING POSITION: Lie on your back with your knees slightly bent and your feet slightly off the ground. Fold your hands by your side (easiest), across your chest or stomach (difficult), or folded behind your head (most difficult). Tuck your chin to your chest and, using your stomach muscles, lift your shoulders off the floor.

EXERCISE PERFORMANCE: Keep your right leg slightly bent and one inch or so off the ground. Bend your left knee and bring the knee toward the head. Raise your head and shoulders off the floor and twist your upper body such that your right elbow moves toward the left knee. Your right elbow should touch your left knee over the middle of the stomach around the belly button area. Hold the position for a count of one, and slowly return to the starting position. Immediately bend the right knee

Figure 6.30 Advanced bicycle.

and bring it toward your stomach, while you raise your upper body off the floor and twist, such that your left elbow touches the right knee. That is one repetition. Your chin should be kept tucked to your chest throughout the entire exercise.

SPECIAL CONSIDERATIONS: This is a difficult exercise to perform unless your stomach muscles are properly prepared. The athlete should be able to perform ten partial curls correctly before using this exercise.

BREATHING: Smoothly exhale as you pull yourself up to touch your elbows to your knee. Inhale as you lower yourself to the starting position.

SPOTTER'S RESPONSIBILITIES: A spotter is not necessary.

THE FINAL REPETITION

We have come to the end of our weight training journey. In the last two chapters we have examined many of the most commonly asked questions, from muscle physiology to the performance of specific exercises. The purpose of these chapters was to provide usable information while dispelling several of the myths that surround the areas of weight training and conditioning.

Throughout this journey I have thought of us as weight training partners. Now it is your turn to perform the exercises. If you have a question, pick up the book and reread the appropriate pages.

A few final reminders:
- Thoroughly read and understand the technique of each exercise.
- Perform each exercise through a full range of motion.
- Always control the weight, do not let the weight control you.
- Always use proper technique.
- Learn the names of the muscles and think about how you are improving your body.
- Weight training is more fun when done with teammates and friends.

Epilogue

Now that you have finished reading the book, let us share with you how we started this project. Three years ago, David Watson organized a conference for coaches and parents on the topic of coaching young athletes. David and Jon Hellstedt gave presentations at the conference. Approximately sixty people attended, and the response was very positive.

Several months later, David organized another workshop, this time with a smaller group of ski instructors and coaches from a nearby ski area. Dan Rooks gave a presentation along with David and Jon. After the workshop the three of us met and evaluated the experience. The feedback we had received was very encouraging. Many people suggested we do more to communicate our philosophy of youth sports participation. At this meeting we decided to put some of our own ideas into book form and seek a publisher. The present volume is an outgrowth from the ideas first presented at these meetings.

We agreed to have Virginia Kimball join us. She had worked with David on some other writing projects and offered us the chance to have a professional writer take our individual contributions and put them together in a literary style that roughly approximated one voice.

We have been working on this book for two years. Frequently we would get together, present our work, and critique each other's contribution. Since we each represent a different scientific discipline, through our collaboration we have learned much from one another.

After we had finished the main content of our chapters, we decided to meet another time, and put together a list of major guidelines that we think parents should follow when supporting and nurturing their children in youth sports.

We have put these guidelines in a format that resembles a list that one of us saw hanging on the wall of a gymnastics training facility. The original author is unknown, and what follows is our own version of the ten basic rules.

The Ten Commandments for Parents of Athletic Children

1. Make sure your children know that, win or lose, you love them and are not disappointed with their performance.
2. Be realistic about your child's physical ability.
3. Help your child set realistic goals.
4. Emphasize improved performance, not winning. Positively reinforce improved skills.
5. Don't relive your own athletic past through your child.
6. Provide a safe environment for your child's training and competition. This includes the proper use of equipment and training methods.
7. Control your own emotions at games and events. Don't yell at other players, coaches, or officials.
8. Be a cheerleader for your child and the other children on the team.
9. Respect your child's coaches. Communicate openly with them. If you disagree with their approach, discuss it with them.
10. Be a positive role model for your child. Enjoy sports yourself. Set your own goals. Live a healthy lifestyle.

We will end our journey with these guidelines. If you follow them, the youth sport experience will provide a rich experience for you and your children.

We believe that sports can help strengthen and preserve the family, promote individual growth and development, and provide an outlet for fun for everyone who participates. We hope this book will help you enjoy the myriad of experiences that youth sports will offer each member of your family.

We also want to know your reactions and questions to the material we have presented. Please use the feedback sheet that follows to write to us with your ideas and questions. We are looking forward to hearing from you.

Questions and Comments

The authors would like to hear from you with your reactions, both positive and negative, to the book. We would also like to know what questions you'd like answered that were not addressed in our book.

Please tear out the sheet and send your thoughts and questions to On the Sidelines, HRD Press, 22 Amherst Rd., Amherst, MA 01002. We will try to respond to your questions by mail, so be sure to list your name and address if you want us to contact you.

1. The things I liked about your book are:

2. The things I didn't like about your book are:

3. The questions I have that I would like you to answer are:

Name _____

Address _____

_____

Index